Edible Wild Mushrooms for Beginners

The Ultimate Guide to Foraging, Growing Gourmet and Medicinal Mushrooms at Home, outdoor and Harvesting Techniques with full color pictures

Ella Grant

Disclaimer

This book is based on the author's experience, research, and opinions. The author does not guarantee or warrant the information, advice, or opinion in this book. The author is not responsible for any errors, omissions, or results from using this information. The author does not endorse or recommend any products, services, or organizations in this book.

The views and opinions in this book are the author's only and not of anyone else. The author is not liable for any damages or losses from using or misusing this book. The reader is responsible for their actions and consequences. The author is not liable for any damages from this book. This book is for information and education only and not for any advice.

The reader should consult a professional before using this information. The author is not a licensed or certified professional. This book is copyrighted and may not be copied or sold without the author's permission.

TABLE OF CONTENT

Introduction

Why Forage for Mushrooms?

Mushrooms are amazing. There are hundreds of different kinds of mushrooms, with an infinite variety of names, tastes, sizes, forms, and uses. Certain mushrooms are tasty and nourishing, while others are rare and amazing, therapeutic and restorative, or just plain entertaining to seek out and locate. Moreover, mushrooms are an essential component of the natural world, serving as key players in the biosphere and ecosystem.

A great way to appreciate the variety and beauty of mushrooms, as well as their culinary and medicinal uses, is to go mushroom foraging. You may explore the outdoors, establish a connection with nature, and discover new aspects of the environment and yourself by going mushroom hunting. Foraging for mushrooms may be a significant and gratifying lifestyle choice, a demanding and thrilling pastime, or both.

The benefits of foraging for mushrooms

Foraging for mushrooms has several advantages, both material and immaterial, social and personal. These are a few of the important ones:

- **You get to enjoy locally grown, organic, and fresh cuisine.** You can get some of the most delicious and nourishing food on the planet—free of pesticides, additives, and packaging—by going mushroom foraging. In addition, you may sample the seasonal and local varieties of mushrooms and explore new tastes and textures. Because some of the most sought-after mushrooms may be quite pricey on the market, foraging for mushrooms can also help you save money.
- **Your emotional and physical well-being both improve.** Finding mushrooms through foraging is an excellent physical and mental workout. By walking, trekking, bending, and crouching in the woods, you may

increase your immune system, burn calories, build your muscles, and enhance your balance. It's also possible to lower stress, improve mood, spark creativity, and hone your senses by taking in the fresh air, spending time in nature, and practicing mindfulness. The health benefits of antioxidants, antibacterial, antiviral, antiparasitic, anticancer, antiallergic, antitumor, analgesic, cardioprotective, and cholesterol-lowering qualities found in some mushrooms may also be obtained via mushroom foraging.

- **You pick up new abilities and information.** A lifetime learning process, mushroom foraging may deepen your awareness of both the natural world and yourself. You may find out how to recognize and stay away from toxic mushrooms, gather, store, and preserve mushrooms, cultivate your own at home, cook and prepare mushrooms in a variety of ways, and utilize mushrooms for medicinal and other uses. Additionally, you may learn about the variety and ecology of mushrooms, as well as their historical and cultural significance, ecological roles and functions, interactions with other creatures, and ties with humans.

- **You make connections with the environment and other people.** One social and environmental activity that might promote a sense of community and responsibility is mushroom foraging. In addition to enjoying the companionship and camaraderie of other mushroom enthusiasts, you may meet and engage with other mushroom enthusiasts, join and contribute to mushroom organizations and events, and share and learn from other mushroom foragers. You may also support and engage in mushroom research and education, preserve and maintain the habitat and population of mushrooms, respect and value the environment, and adhere to and promote the ethics and etiquette of foraging.

The challenges and risks of foraging for mushrooms

There are hazards and difficulties associated with mushroom foraging, both social and personal, small and large. These are a few of the important ones:

- **You can come upon hazardous or toxic mushrooms.** Because many mushrooms are toxic or hazardous and may cause anything from slight pain to severe disease or even death, mushroom foraging takes caution and attention. There are many types of mushrooms:

poisonous, hallucinogenic, allergic, toxic, and just plain ugly. Certain mushrooms are simple to recognize, while others are difficult, changeable, and deceiving. Certain mushrooms have delayed symptoms, limited treatment options, no antidote, and cumulative effects. It takes expertise, experience, common sense, and sound judgment to forage mushrooms.

- **You can get into moral or legal problems.** Laws, rules, morality, and etiquette all apply to mushroom foraging, and they might change depending on the circumstance, destination, and goal. Certain locations have quotas or limitations; some have fees or penalties, some ban or restrict mushroom harvesting; and others need licenses or approvals. There are those who like or encourage mushroom foraging, those who reject or condemn it, those who compete with or have conflicts with it, and others who take advantage of or misuse mushroom foraging. In addition to knowledge and compliance, foraging for mushrooms also calls for civility and respect.

- **There might be obstacles or risks.** It's not always simple or safe to forage for mushrooms since there are a lot of obstacles to overcome and risks associated with the weather, animals, environment, and even oneself. Certain locations are busy or competitive; others are contaminated or difficult to get to; some are protected or limited; and yet others are congested or difficult to traverse. There are many types of weather conditions: unpleasant or unexpected, dangerous or harsh, demanding or constantly changing, and limiting or restricting. Certain animals are aggressive or menacing, while others are dangerous or lethal. Some animals are benign or amiable, while others are bothersome or unpleasant. Situations may be classified as follows: some are dangerous or frightening, others are unpleasant or uncomfortable, and some are emergency or life-threatening. In addition to readiness and prudence, foraging for mushrooms calls for flexibility and resiliency.

The ethics and etiquette of foraging for mushrooms

In addition to being a solitary hobby, mushroom foraging also benefits the environment and society. Respecting and preserving the natural resources that we use and enjoy is a shared duty among foragers. Therefore, in order to promote a sustainable and peaceful activity, it is crucial to adhere to a few fundamental ethical and etiquette guidelines while mushroom-foraging. These are a few of the important ones:

- **Know your stuff, and be ready.** Make sure you know all there is to know about the many kinds of mushrooms in your region, including their seasons, habitats, and traits, before you go mushroom hunting. Know which ones are toxic and edible, and don't choose any that you are unsure about. To expand your knowledge and experience, consult reputable field guides, websites, or specialists. You may also attend seminars or join groups. Additionally, learn about the rules and legislation pertaining to foraging in your area and get any required licenses or authorizations. Pack the necessary tools and supplies, such as a GPS unit, a map, a compass, a basket, a knife, and a brush. Carry adequate food and drink, and dress for the terrain and the weather. Have a strategy in place for safely returning to your vehicle or house in case of an emergency or other unforeseen circumstance.

- **Act civil and polite.** When you go foraging, be mindful of the surrounding environment and be kind to everyone you come across. Don't forget to "Leave No Trace" and try to make as little of an impression as possible. Follow designated trails and routes; do not stomp on or harm the soil or plants. Always pack out what you bring in, and avoid leaving any trash or litter behind. Take caution while harvesting mushrooms so as not to disrupt the spores or the mycelium. Don't overharvest or discard any mushrooms; instead, leave some for the ecology and other foragers. Respect the rights and desires of the landowners or management, and refrain from trespassing on private or protected areas. Remember to stay away from any possible risks or hazards, and do not tamper with or injure any animals. Treat fellow foragers, hikers, and tourists with courtesy and friendliness, and avoid causing any disputes or issues. Talk about your love and expertise for mushrooms, but don't tell anybody where your hidden areas are or assume that others will. Don't gloat or brag about your discoveries; instead, be modest and appreciative of nature's offerings.

- **Be responsible and safe.** Although it may be lucrative and enjoyable, mushroom foraging can also be perilous and deadly. As a result, it's essential to take care of others as well as oneself while foraging and to act safely and responsibly. Foraging should always be done in pairs, or you should notify someone of your whereabouts and anticipated return time. Keep a first aid kit, radio, mobile phone, flashlight, whistle, and knowledge of how to utilize them with you at all times. Keep an eye out for any potential threats or impediments, like dangerous plants, insects, snakes, bears, cliffs, rivers, etc. Never go foraging while you're dehydrated, fatigued, hungry, or intoxicated. Never ingest mushrooms that are rotting, old, or tainted, nor should you eat any that you are unsure about. Get medical help right away if you suffer any poisoning symptoms, such as nausea, vomiting, diarrhea, dizziness, etc., and don't forget to bring a sample of the mushroom you consumed. Be truthful and responsible for your deeds, and refrain from blaming or suing other people for your errors or bad luck.

The tools and equipment for foraging for mushrooms

Although hardly much gear is needed for mushroom foraging, having some may improve the efficiency and enjoyment of the process. The following are some of the necessary supplies and gear for mushroom foraging:

- **A mesh bag or a basket.** The most crucial instrument for mushroom gathering is this one. The mushrooms can breathe and are kept from being damaged or crushed by using a mesh bag or basket. It also facilitates the spores' dissemination and the mushroom's growth. A plastic bag may trap heat and moisture, causing the mushrooms to rot or deteriorate. Instead, use a mesh bag or a basket. Your harvest should fit into a basket or mesh bag, but it shouldn't be too big or heavy to transport. Additionally, it needs to feature a handle or strap that is easy to grip.

- **A blade.** When collecting mushrooms, particularly those with stiff or woody stems, a knife is needed. Cutting the mushrooms at their base with a knife can help you prevent pulling or digging them out. You may clean the mushrooms with a knife by scraping off any dirt, debris, or insects. A knife needs to be simple to use, strong, and sharp. The perfect knife is a pocket knife or a mushroom knife with a curved blade and brush. A knife should also have a cover or sheath to safeguard the blade and shield users from harm or mishaps.

- **A bristle brush.** Cleaning mushrooms and getting rid of any dirt, debris, or insects may be done using a brush. By using a brush, you may prevent the mushrooms from becoming soggy or slimy by not washing them with water, which will maintain their texture and form. A brush may be used alone or as an attachment for your knife. A brush needs to be mild, soft, and efficient. A toothbrush or a boar's hair brush works well. Additionally, a brush has to be hygienic, clean, and free of pollutants or diseases that might infect the mushrooms.

- **a shovel.** When digging out mushrooms, particularly ones that grow partly underground, like truffles or puffballs, a shovel comes in handy. You may remove the mushrooms and their mycelium without harming them by using a trowel to break up the dirt. After harvesting, a trowel may also be used to rehabilitate the soil by filling up the holes. A trowel must be compact, lightweight, and sturdy. It's acceptable to use a folding trowel or a gardening trowel. A trowel needs to be safe for the environment and you, as well as clean and sharp.

- **a field manual.** To identify mushrooms in the outdoors and tell the difference between edible and deadly ones, a field guide is essential. Every mushroom should have crisp, detailed photos and descriptions in a field guide, together with information on its common and scientific names, habitat, season, traits, toxicity, edibility, and confusions. A field guide should also include identifying advice and techniques for mushrooms, such as taste and smell, spore prints, and chemical testing. A field guide needs to be trustworthy, thorough, and current. In addition, a field guide needs to be waterproof, lightweight, and readable.

- **A guide.** Finding your way in and out of the woods and maintaining direction are two things that a compass may aid with. You can prevent becoming lost or confused by using a compass to find your house, vehicle, or mushroom locations. You may record your routes and locations and mark your paths using a compass. A compass needs to be reliable, practical, and simple to use. It works quite nicely to use a digital or magnetic compass. In addition, a compass needs to be easily observable, safe, and unbreakable.

* **a headlight.** For illumination, visibility, and seeing in dim or dark environments, a headlamp is helpful. Using a light may help you find mushrooms, particularly those that are concealed or disguised, and prevent you from missing out on opportunities or hidden gems. You can see your surroundings and steer clear of any obstructions or risks with the aid of a light. A headlight needs to be comfortable, bright, and adaptable. It's best to use a rechargeable or LED headlamp. In addition to being strong, waterproof, and battery-operated, a headlamp should also not malfunction or run out of juice.

The history and evolution of mushroom foraging

The act of seeking out, gathering, and ingesting wild mushrooms for sustenance, medicinal purposes, or recreational purposes is known as mushroom foraging. Foraging for mushrooms has a long and intriguing history that probably began in antiquity when different societies realized the possibilities of fungus. The practice of mushroom foraging has changed throughout time in response to social, cultural, and environmental influences, as well as to showcase the variety and inventiveness of interactions between humans and mushrooms. The following aspects of the development and history of mushroom foraging will be examined in this chapter:

- The origins and evidence of mushroom foraging
- The cultural and regional variations of mushroom foraging
- The techniques and tools of mushroom foraging
- The myths and legends of mushroom foraging

The origins and evidence of mushroom foraging

Although the history of mushroom foraging is unknown, it is thought that people have been gathering mushrooms for thousands of years—possibly even before the beginning of civilization. Archaeological, historical, and artistic sources provide the oldest known accounts of mushroom harvesting, indicating that ancient peoples, including the Egyptians, Greeks, Romans, Chinese, and Indians, were acquainted with and used a variety of mushroom species. Several indications of prehistoric mushroom harvesting include:

- Egyptian hieroglyphs: In their hieroglyphic writing, which dates back to about BC, the ancient Egyptians portrayed mushrooms. Pharaohs and nobles were the only ones allowed to possess mushrooms since they were thought to bring immortality. In addition, the Egyptians used mushrooms as a medicine to cure diseases and wounds.

- Greek and Roman writings: In their literature and philosophy, which go back to about BC, the ancient Greeks and Romans discussed mushrooms. In addition to appreciating mushrooms' flavor and nutritional worth, the Greeks and Romans were aware of their toxic and hallucinogenic qualities. In addition, mushrooms were employed for religious and ceremonial reasons by the Greeks and Romans, who offered them to the gods and used them for divination.

- The Chinese paintings: dating back to about BC, the ancient Chinese painted mushrooms. The Chinese regarded mushrooms as emblems of longevity and wisdom and held them in high regard for their therapeutic and spiritual properties. As early as AD, the Chinese began cultivating mushrooms, including shiitake and oyster mushrooms.

- Indian sculptures: From about BC, the ancient Indians portrayed mushrooms in their sculptures. The medicinal and illuminating properties of mushrooms were highly treasured by the Indians, who also connected them to holy plants and animals. In addition, the Indians used psilocybe and amanita mushrooms for religious and ceremonial reasons, including trance states and visions.

The cultural and regional variations of mushroom foraging

Depending on the variety and availability of mushrooms, local customs and beliefs, historical and environmental factors, and local conditions, mushroom foraging has taken on many forms across cultures and geographical areas. The social and cultural identities and values of the mushroom foragers, as well as the interactions and connections between people and fungus, have all been expressed in mushroom foraging. The following are some examples of how mushroom foraging varies by culture and region:

- The variety and distribution of mushrooms, as well as the foragers' tastes and methods, have been impacted by Europe's climate, geography, and history. These factors have also had an impact on European mushroom foraging. The European culinary and medical traditions, which have used mushrooms in a variety of foods and treatments, have also had an impact on European mushroom foraging. The European mythology and folklore, which give different powers and meanings to mushrooms, have also had an impact on the practice of mushroom harvesting. Here are a few instances of European mushroom foraging:

- The rich and diverse food of France, which has embraced mushrooms as delicacies and specialties, has had an effect on the art of French mushroom foraging. The rural and pastoral culture of France, which has promoted a strong relationship and enjoyment of nature and fungus, has also had an impact on French mushroom foraging. The geographical and seasonal variances of France have also affected French mushroom foraging, producing a variety of mushroom kinds and numbers as well as mushroom-related festivals and events.

- German mushroom hunting: Germany's hilly and wooded terrain, which offers a favorable and plentiful environment for mushrooms, has an impact on the country's mushroom hunting practices. The practical and scientific attitude of Germany, which has placed an emphasis on the identification and categorization of mushrooms as well as the prevention and treatment of mushroom poisoning, has also had an impact on German mushroom foraging. The social and recreational aspects of German culture have also affected mushroom foraging, since mushroom foraging has been promoted as a family pastime and leisure activity.

o The broad and seasonal variety of mushrooms found in Italy is a result of the country's Mediterranean and Alpine environment, which has affected the art of mushroom harvesting. The geographical and cultural variety of Italy has also had an impact on mushroom foraging, leading to variations in the names and applications of mushrooms as well as in laws and limitations surrounding mushroom foraging. The cultural and aesthetic sensibility of Italy has also affected Italian mushroom harvesting, serving as an inspiration for the production of mushroom-related crafts including jewelry, paintings, and sculptures.

- North American mushroom foraging: From the temperate woods of the east to the dry deserts of the west, North America's large and diverse topography and ecology have supplied a broad and rich range of mushrooms, which have impacted North American mushroom foraging. The indigenous and immigrant cultures of North America, from the Native American tribes to the European settlers, have all contributed to and shared their knowledge and customs about mushrooms, which has had an impact on North American mushroom foraging. The contemporary and inventive tendencies in North America have also had an impact on mushroom foraging, leading to new initiatives and advancements in the field, such as mushroom farms, festivals, and clubs.

- The tropical and subtropical environment of Asia has encouraged the development and variety of mushrooms, particularly in the jungles and wetlands of Southeast Asia. This has had an impact on the practice of Asian mushroom foraging. Asian traditional and holistic philosophies have also impacted Asian mushroom harvesting. These philosophies have long recognized the therapeutic and spiritual benefits of mushrooms and have included them in a variety of systems and practices, including traditional Chinese medicine, Ayurveda, and Buddhism. The unusual and daring Asian cuisines, which have used mushrooms in a variety of meals and treats, including soups, stir-fries, and sushi, have also had an impact on Asian mushroom hunting.

The techniques and tools of mushroom foraging

With the creation and advancement of several methods and equipment that have increased the effectiveness and security of mushroom foraging, mushroom foraging has changed over time. The methods and equipment used for mushroom foraging have also changed based on the kind and location of mushrooms, the goals and tastes of the foragers, and the resources' accessibility and availability. Among the methods and equipment used in mushroom foraging are:

- The methods for classifying and identifying mushrooms are crucial for mushroom foraging because they enable the distinction of beneficial and edible mushrooms from toxic and inedible ones, as well as the understanding of the traits and qualities of various species and kinds of mushrooms. The methods used to identify and classify mushrooms have changed over time. Traditional, empirical methods like looking at the morphology, anatomy, color, smell, taste, or habitat of the mushrooms have given way to more modern, scientific methods like using chemistry, microscopy, genetics, or the phylogeny of mushrooms. Techniques for identifying and classifying mushrooms have also been supported by a variety of tools and resources, including specialists, field guides, keys, books, websites, and applications.

- The methods for harvesting and gathering mushrooms are: These methods are crucial to mushroom foraging because they reduce harm and disruption to the mushrooms and their environments while also assisting in the acquisition and preservation of a high-quality and plentiful supply of mushrooms. Techniques for harvesting and gathering mushrooms have developed throughout time, moving from basic manual methods like digging, chopping, or picking them by hand to more sophisticated mechanical ways like harvesting and collecting mushrooms using rakes, knives, scissors, or trowels. Various tools and equipment, including baskets, bags, boxes, or containers to store and transport mushrooms, have also assisted in the gathering and collection of mushrooms.

- The methods for cleaning and processing mushrooms are helpful for mushroom foraging since they aid in clearing the mushrooms of dirt and impurities as well as preparing and preserving them for use or eating. Techniques for cleaning and processing mushrooms have developed throughout time, moving from simple, natural processes like brushing, washing, or drying them in the sun, air, or water to more sophisticated, man-made processes like soaking, peeling, or freezing them using chemicals, equipment, or electricity. The cleaning and processing of mushrooms have also been made easier by the use of a variety of equipment, including brushes, knives, peelers, and freezers.

The myths and legends of mushroom foraging

Foraging for mushrooms has been enhanced by a sense of mystery and wonder due to the many tales and legends surrounding it. Various societies have long held mushrooms in high regard and mythologized them, often connecting them to stories of mystique, magic, and even heavenly beginnings. Here are a few myths and tales around mushroom foraging:

- The fairy rings are circular mushroom formations that may be found in forests, meadows, and other types of environments. Fairy rings, so the legend goes, are the locations where fairies and other otherworldly creatures gathered, danced, and feasted at night, leaving behind mushrooms as a memento of their presence. In addition, fairy rings are said to possess a variety of magical abilities, depending on how they are approached or entered, including the ability to fulfill wishes, confer luck, or bring calamity.

- The fly agaric: This particular kind of mushroom has a characteristic red cap speckled with white. It is also among the most toxic and hallucinogenic mushrooms, with psychoactive chemicals that may produce a range of symptoms, including delirium, euphoria, and hallucinations. Fly agaric has been associated with many myths and stories, including the story of Santa Claus's beginnings, Alice in Wonderland's inspiration, and the holy mushroom of the Indo-Europeans of old.

- The soma: Described in India's ancient Vedic scriptures from about BC, the soma is a mystery plant or substance. The gods and priests were said to imbibe soma, a heavenly and intoxicating beverage that conferred diverse advantages, including health, pleasure, or enlightenment. Many other plants and substances have been proposed as the source of Soma, but the most widely accepted theory is that it was a kind of mushroom, either the psilocybe or the fly agaric kind.

- Ergot is a kind of fungus that may infect rye, wheat, and barley, among other cereals. It creates alkaloids, which may result in a variety of symptoms, including gangrene, hallucinations, or convulsions. Ergot has been connected to a number of historical occurrences and events, including the French Revolution, the origins of LSD, and the Salem witch trials.

The current trends and challenges in the field of mushroom foraging

In this chapter, we will explore the following aspects of the current trends and challenges in the field of mushroom foraging:

- The increasing popularity and demand for mushroom foraging
- The rising awareness and education of mushroom foraging
- The expanding diversity and innovation of mushroom foraging
- The persisting risks and threats of mushroom foraging
- The emerging opportunities and solutions of mushroom foraging

The increasing popularity and demand for mushroom foraging

Since more people are becoming aware of the advantages and joys of mushroom foraging, mushroom foraging has grown in popularity and demand in recent years. The following are some of the elements that have led to the growing demand for and popularity of mushroom foraging:

- The nutritional value and health advantages of mushrooms: Packed with different proteins, vitamins, minerals, antioxidants, and other bioactive components, mushrooms are a tasty and healthy dietary source. In addition, mushrooms have been shown to strengthen immunity, reduce cholesterol, and either prevent or cure a number of illnesses, including diabetes, hypertension, and cancer.

- The therapeutic and medical advantages of mushrooms: A rich and useful source of medicinal chemicals, mushrooms may generate a wide range of substances or compounds with pharmacological effects, including antibacterial, antifungal, antiviral, anti-inflammatory, immunomodulatory, and anticancer properties. In addition, mushrooms have a number of medical and therapeutic uses, including the treatment of infections, wounds, and inflammations, as well as improvements to mood, clarity of thought, and general wellbeing.

- The gastronomic and culinary advantages of mushrooms: Delicious and adaptable, mushrooms may be used in a wide range of recipes and treats, including soups, salads, stir-fries, and pizzas. Additionally, mushrooms may improve the taste, texture, or look of food as well as provide diversity, originality, or innovation to culinary preparations.

- The advantages of mushrooms in terms of enjoyment and experiences: Food sources that are entertaining and delightful to eat for discovery, adventure, or enjoyment include mushrooms. Additionally, mushrooms may be used recreationally and for a variety of experiences, including boosting the senses, emotions, or imagination and causing hallucinations, altered states of consciousness, or visions.

Foragers, mushrooms, and the environment are facing a number of possibilities and difficulties as a result of the growing demand and popularity of mushroom foraging. For instance, the growing demand and popularity of mushroom foraging have improved the foragers' standard of living and income, but they have also increased the strain and competition on the ecology and the mushrooms themselves.

The rising awareness and education of mushroom foraging

In recent years, as more people have become aware of the ramifications and elements of mushroom foraging, there has been an increase in awareness and education around the practice. The following are some of the elements that have led to an increase in mushroom foraging knowledge and awareness:

- The developments in science and technology related to mushroom foraging: The advancements in science and technology that have enhanced the identification, categorization, production, and processing of mushrooms have been beneficial to mushroom foraging. For instance, the accuracy and dependability of mushroom identification and categorization have increased with the use of microscopy, chemistry, genetics, and phylogeny. The processing and production of mushrooms are now more safe and efficient thanks to the use of equipment, gadgets, and applications.

- The social and cultural exchanges that accompany mushroom foraging include: The knowledge and customs around mushrooms have been transmitted and propagated via social and cultural exchanges, which has helped mushroom foraging. For instance, media, websites, and books have all been used to spread knowledge and education about mushrooms. Foragers for mushrooms have found it easier to communicate and connect with one another thanks to clubs, festivals, and tours.

- The awareness of the environment and ecology surrounding mushroom foraging: The protection and care of mushrooms and their habitats have been increased and encouraged by environmental and ecological awareness around mushroom foraging. For instance, the status and trends of mushrooms and their habitats have been identified and assessed via the use of data, indicators, and monitoring. The mushrooms and their habitats have been preserved and controlled by the application of laws, rules, and standards.

Growing public knowledge and education of mushroom foraging has brought out a range of possibilities as well as difficulties for the environment, the mushrooms, and the foragers. For instance, greater knowledge and education about mushroom foraging has improved the safety and quality of the mushrooms, but it has also raised standards and expectations for both the environment and the foragers.

The expanding diversity and innovation of mushroom foraging

In recent times, there has been an increase in the diversity and inventiveness of mushroom foraging, as more individuals have been delving further into the possible benefits of this practice. The following are a few elements that support the growing variety and inventiveness of mushroom foraging:

- The availability and accessibility of mushroom foraging: As more individuals are able to access and afford the possibilities and resources associated with mushroom foraging, mushroom foraging has become more accessible and available. For instance, the growth and development of the infrastructure, communication, and transportation related to mushroom foraging have enhanced the availability and accessibility of mushroom foraging. The growth and diversity of the markets for mushroom foraging-related goods and services have also led to a rise in the availability and accessibility of mushroom foraging.

- The novelty and diversity of mushroom foraging: As more people learn about and appreciate the inventiveness and diversity of mushroom foraging, it has become a more diversified and unique activity. For instance, the discovery and introduction of new kinds and species of mushrooms, such as exotic, uncommon, or therapeutic mushrooms, has expanded the diversity and novelty of mushroom hunting. The exploration and development of new mushroom foraging methods and techniques, such as vertical, indoor, and urban foraging, has also led to a rise in the diversity and novelty of mushroom foraging.

- The ability to pick and adjust one's tastes and experiences with mushroom foraging has allowed for a greater degree of personalization and customization of the activity. For instance, the differentiation and segmentation of the foragers, mushrooms, and ecosystems depending on numerous variables, such as age, gender, location, or goal, has expanded the personalization and customization of mushroom foraging. Due to the adaptability and optimization of the foraging process and result depending on several parameters, such as season, weather, or quality, the personalization and customization of mushroom foraging have also risen.

There are now more possibilities and difficulties for foragers, mushrooms, and the ecology as a result of the growing variety and inventiveness of mushroom foraging. For instance, the growing variety and inventiveness of mushroom foraging have raised the pleasure and worth of the mushrooms, but they have also made the procedure and results more complicated and unpredictable.

The persisting risks and threats of mushroom foraging

In recent times, mushroom foraging has encountered a range of dangers and obstacles due to increased public awareness of the associated challenges and hazards. Several elements are involved in the ongoing dangers and concerns associated with mushroom harvesting. These include:

- The poisoning and contamination of mushrooms: Because mushrooms may result in a variety of negative symptoms, including nausea, vomiting, diarrhea, and even death, mushroom poisoning and contamination pose significant dangers and threats to mushroom gathering. Ingesting toxic or uneatable mushrooms or exposing them to pollutants or contaminants like pesticides, herbicides, fertilizers, heavy metals, or radioactive materials may result in mushroom contamination and poisoning.

- The health and production of mushrooms may be affected by illnesses and pests, which make them frequent dangers and threats to mushroom foraging. Many creatures that may infect, harm, or kill mushrooms or their environments, including fungus, bacteria, viruses, insects, nematodes, or mites, can be the source of mushroom diseases and pests. Numerous elements, including wind, water, animals, and people, may potentially transfer or spread pests and illnesses associated with mushrooms.

- The rivalry and conflict surrounding mushroom foraging: Since these factors have the potential to impact mushroom abundance and accessibility, they provide hazards and dangers to mushroom foraging. Competition and conflict among mushrooms may arise from differences in mushroom abundance or scarcity, as well as from similarities or differences among foragers. Conflicts and rivalry over the rights, interests, or values of mushroom foragers, such as ownership, use, or conservation, may also arise.

Foragers, mushrooms, and the environment as a whole face a number of difficulties and issues as a result of the ongoing dangers and hazards associated with mushroom foraging. For instance, the ongoing dangers and hazards associated with mushroom foraging have reduced the quality and safety of mushrooms while simultaneously raising demand and the need for risk and threat management and mitigation.

Part 1: The Basics of Mushroom Foraging

Chapter 1: What are Mushrooms and How Do They Grow?

Fascinating creatures, mushrooms are members of the fungal world. They possess traits of both plants and animals, yet they are neither of them. They lack chlorophyll and photosynthesis, although they are made of cells with nuclei and cell walls. They lack tissues and organs while being multicellular and eukaryotic. Because they are saprophytic and heterotrophic, they get their nutrition and energy from organic materials like dead plants and animals.

Although they are the visible and edible portions of certain fungi, mushrooms are not the whole fungus. Spores are tiny seeds produced by fungus, and these reproductive structures are responsible for producing and releasing them. The spores may germinate and develop into new mushrooms under the right circumstances. They are dispersed by the wind, water, or animals. Although they are not the sole means, spores are the primary means by which fungi proliferate and diversify. Asexual means of reproduction for some fungi include vegetative growth, budding, and fragmentation.

The anatomy and biology of mushrooms

The biology of mushrooms is intricate and dynamic, despite their simple and exquisite morphology. The mycelium and the fruiting body are their two basic components. The portion of the fungus that we see and consume is called the fruiting body, while the portion that is invisible to us but vital to its life and expansion is called the mycelium.

The Fruiting Body

The structure that holds and distributes the spores is called the fruiting body, often referred to as the sporocarp or the mushroom. Its typical structure consists of a cap and a stem, but it may also include other characteristics like teeth, rings, veils, gills, holes, or volvas. Mushroom species vary greatly in their form, size, color, texture, and arrangement of these characteristics, all of which may be used to identify and categorize the species.

The top portion of the fruiting body that covers and shields the area that produces spores is called the cap, or pileus. The cap's surfaces might be smooth, scaly, warty, hairy, or irregular. It can also be flat, convex, conical, bell-shaped, or uneven. Depending on the species and age of the mushroom, the cap may also have distinct colors, patterns, or markings. The cap may be free of the stem or fastened to it via a central, eccentric, or lateral point.

The portion of the fruiting body that produces and releases spores is called the spore-producing surface, or hymenium. The bottom of the cap, the sides, or the top of the fruiting body might all be considered the spore-producing surface. The surface that produces spores may take on many shapes, including tubes, gills, holes, and teeth. From the stem to the edge of the cap, the gills are thin, plate-like structures. The surface of the fruiting body is covered with tiny, angular, or circular holes. The teeth are projections that dangle from the surface of the fruiting body and resemble needles, spines, or elongated structures. The fruiting body's flesh contains cylindrical, hollow, or labyrinthine structures called tubes.

The tiny, unicellular reproductive units of fungi are called spores. Numerous processes, including wind, rain, insects, and animals, release the spores into the air or water when they are created in significant quantities by the spore-producing surface. Based on the species and staining technique, the spores may have a variety of colors, sizes, and ornamentations in addition to their typical spherical, oval, or elliptical form. Additionally, the number of nuclei in the spores may vary, from one (haploid) to four (tetraploid).

The portion of the fruiting body that lifts and supports the cap is called the stem, often referred to as the stipe. The stem may vary in length, breadth, form, and texture, and it can be central, eccentric, lateral, or nonexistent. Additionally, the stem may have various characteristics, like a bulb, ring, veil, or volva. The ring, sometimes called the annulus, is a piece of the partial veil, a thin membrane that covers a juvenile mushroom's pores or gills. The ring may have many locations, forms, and textures in addition to being either permanent, transient, or nonexistent. Young mushrooms have a veil, sometimes called a cortina, which is a web-like or cobwebby tissue that joins the cap and stem. A partial veil would just cover the pores or gills, but a global veil would cover the whole fruiting body. The veil may have various colors, patterns, or consistencies and can be either permanent, ephemeral, or nonexistent. The volva, often referred to as the cup, is a piece of the thick membrane that surrounds the whole fruiting body of young mushrooms, known as the universal veil. The volva comes in a variety of sizes, forms, and textures and might resemble a bag, cup, or collar. The bulb, often referred to as the basal bulb, is an inflated or swollen base of the stem that may be indicative of a volva.

The portion of the fruiting body that fills the cap and stem is referred to as the flesh, or context. The species and age of the mushroom may affect the flesh's colors, textures, tastes, scents, and responses. Additionally, the flesh may have layers such as the medulla, cuticle, pileipellis, or trama. The outermost layer of the cap is called the cuticle, or pellicle, and may be hairy, scaly, smooth, or warty. The layer of tissue covering the cuticle, which may be cellular, filamentous, or gelatinous, is called the pileipellis, or cap skin. The primary tissue that fills the cap and stem is called the trama, or flesh proper. It may be homogenous, heterogeneous, or zonate. The center of the stem, often referred to as the medulla, may be packed, hollow, or solid.

The Mycelium

The portion of the fungus that develops and resides in the substrate—such as soil, wood, or organic matter—is called the mycelium, often referred to as the vegetative body or the thallus. Normally imperceptible to the unaided eye, the mycelium sometimes takes the form of mats or threads that are white, yellow, or brown in color. Hyphae, which are minute, tubular, filamentous structures that branch and merge to create a network, make up the mycelium. The fundamental building blocks of fungal structure and function, hyphae are in charge of absorbing nutrients, moving water, and generating enzymes.

There are several varieties of hyphae, including generative and skeletal, monokaryotic and dikaryotic, septate and aseptate. The septate hyphae are divided into segments, each of which contains one or more nuclei, by cross-walls known as septa. The aseptate hyphae feature a continuous cytoplasm with many nuclei and no septa. The monokaryotic hyphae are typically haploid and contain just one nucleus per segment. The dikaryotic hyphae are often diploid and contain two nuclei per segment—one from each parent. The generative hyphae, which are involved in growth and reproduction, are branched, thin, and flexible. The thick, unbranched, stiff skeletal hyphae serve as support and defense structures.

Mycelium may perform symbiotic, parasitic, or saprotrophic roles, among others. The saprotrophic mycelium is crucial to the breakdown and cycling of nutrients because it feeds on dead or decaying organic waste. The parasite mycelium damages or causes illnesses to people, animals, or plants because it feeds on living things. Living in coexistence with other creatures, the symbiotic mycelium may have mutualistic, commensal, or antagonistic interactions. Mycorrhizae, which create advantageous alliances with plant roots, and lichens, which combine to form composite creatures with algae or cyanobacteria, are two instances of symbiotic mycelium.

The ecology and diversity of mushrooms

The fruiting structures of certain fungi that generate spores for reproduction are called mushrooms. They are members of the fungi kingdom of life, which is distinct from both plants and animals. The ecology of mushrooms is varied and intriguing, including a range of functions and interactions with other living things as well as the surrounding environment. We shall examine the following aspects of mushroom ecology in this chapter:

- The diversity and distribution of mushrooms
- The ecological roles and functions of mushrooms
- The ecological interactions and relationships of mushrooms
- The ecological threats and challenges of mushrooms
- The ecological benefits and opportunities of mushrooms

The diversity and distribution of mushrooms

Among the most varied and common creatures on Earth are mushrooms. They offer a diverse spectrum of nutritional advantages and ecological purposes, and they are available in an array of forms, sizes, colors, and textures. While some mushrooms are abundant and straightforward to locate, others are elusive and unusual. While some mushrooms are strange and exquisite, others are straightforward and unremarkable. While some mushrooms are toxic and lethal, others are tasty and edible. While some mushrooms are wild and free, others are domesticated and grown.

The most recent estimates place the number of fungal species in the globe at around. million, with approximately, of those species known to produce mushrooms. These figures might, however, alter with more study and discovery, particularly in the tropics and other uncharted areas. The taxonomic categorization of mushrooms, which is based on their appearance, anatomy, genetics, and phylogeny, reflects the variety of these organisms. The Ascomycota and the Basidiomycota are the two main categories of mushrooms, and they are identified by the spores they generate and the structures that support them. Ascospores are made by the Ascomycota in structures that look like sacs and are called asci. Basidiospores are made by the Basidiomycota on structures that look like clubs and are called basidia. There are several subgroups, orders, families, genera, and species of mushrooms within these groupings, each with unique traits and attributes.

Numerous elements, including soil, vegetation, height, latitude, season, and human activity, affect the dispersion of mushrooms. Almost every ecosystem and habitat on Earth, including the polar and tropical zones, mountains and seas, forests and deserts, and rural and urban places, has the presence of mushrooms. On the other hand, certain mushrooms are endemic, or limited to particular areas or regions, and some have particular needs and preferences for their development and survival. Certain mushrooms, like the snow mushroom Flammulina populicola, which grows on poplar trees in the Arctic, are, for instance, suited to cold and dry environments. Certain mushrooms, like the bioluminescent Mycena chlorophos that shines in the dark in Southeast Asian tropical woods, are acclimated to hot and muggy environments. Certain mushrooms, like the caterpillar fungus Ophiocordyceps sinensis, which parasitizes and mummifies insect larvae on the Tibetan Plateau, are acclimated to high elevations. Certain mushrooms, like the enormous puffball Calvatia gigantea, which may reach a diameter of up to cm in temperate parts of North America and Europe, are suited to low latitudes. Certain mushrooms have a specific season, such as the morel Morchella esculenta, which grows in hardwood woods in North America and Europe and blooms in the spring. Certain mushrooms, like the bracket fungus Ganoderma lucidum, are perennial and may survive for many years on living or dead trees in different parts of the globe.

The ecological roles and functions of mushrooms

Through their interactions with other creatures and the environment, mushrooms perform a variety of significant and varied roles and activities in the ecosystem, both directly and indirectly. Among the roles and functions that mushrooms play in the environment are:

- Decomposition: In ecology, mushrooms are the main organisms that break down organic materials, including wood, leaves, and animal corpses. They release digestive enzymes into the substrate, which reduce the substrate's complex organic compounds to simpler forms that the hyphae can ingest. After being ingested, the molecules are either utilized to create new fungal biomass or to provide energy for the fungus to grow and reproduce. Mushroom decomposition contributes to the ecosystem's ability to recycle carbon and nutrients and to keep the carbon and nutrient cycles intact.

- Symbiosis: In the environment, mushrooms form several symbiotic partnerships with various creatures, including plants, animals, and other fungi. Benefits like nutrition, water, shelter, or dispersion are traded with their partners. Mushroom symbiosis contributes to the stability and variety of the environment by promoting the development and survival of both partners. Typical forms of symbiosis using mushrooms include the following:

- o A symbiotic association known as mycorrhiza occurs when a fungus and a plant work together to help the plant collect nutrients and water from the soil. The plant gives the fungus organic carbon via photosynthesis. Mycorrhiza is widely distributed and vital to the health and development of the majority of plants in the environment, particularly trees.

- o Lichen: A symbiotic connection in which a fungus and a photosynthetic partner, such as an alga or cyanobacterium, cooperate to produce organic carbon for the fungus via photosynthesis and protection for the partner. In the ecosystem, lichen is a special and varied collection of organisms that can colonize and survive in hard and severe conditions like rocks, bark, or dirt.

- o Endophyte: A symbiotic relationship in which a fungus lives inside a plant without harming it and benefits the plant in a variety of ways, such as increased resistance to pathogens, pests, drought, or salinity. This relationship can occur in the tissues of a plant, such as the leaves, stems, or seeds. Endophyte is a frequent and pervasive phenomenon that has an impact on the ecology and physiology of many different plants in the environment, particularly grasses.

- Parasitism: In the ecosystem, mushrooms are involved in a variety of parasitic interactions with other creatures, including animals, plants, and other fungi. They injure or even kill their hosts in exchange for nutrition and energy. In addition to generating new possibilities and niches for other creatures in the environment, parasitism by mushrooms aids in the regulation of host population and variety. Several well-known forms of parasitism that affect mushrooms include:
  - Rust: A fungal-plant parasitic connection in which the fungus infects the plant and produces spores that generate pustules or rust-colored patches on the plant's leaves, stems, or fruits. Rust is a dangerous and pervasive disease that impacts a broad range of crops in the environment, including soybeans, maize, and wheat.

o Cordyceps: An insect and fungus have a parasitic relationship in which the fungus infects the insect, takes control of its body and behavior, and finally develops into a fruiting body that protrudes from the insect's head or body. A unique and varied class of fungus known as cordyceps is capable of controlling and manipulating the thoughts and behaviors of a wide range of insects found in the environment, including ants, caterpillars, and beetles.

o Chytrid: A parasitic association in which a fungus infects the skin of an amphibian, such as a salamander, toad, or frog, and results in the deadly illness known as chytridiomycosis. Numerous amphibian species, particularly frogs, have declined or gone extinct as a result of the severe and new danger known as chytrid.

The ecological interactions and relationships of mushrooms

Depending on the kind and form of the connection and contact, mushrooms may have both beneficial and negative effects on other living things as well as the environment. Among the linkages and interactions that mushrooms have in their ecosystem are:

- Competition is the interaction and connection between two or more organisms that negatively impacts each other's ability to develop and survive in the environment by sharing the same or comparable resources, such as nutrients, water, space, or light. When mushrooms compete with other fungus or other creatures for the same or comparable substrates or habitats within the ecosystem, competition takes place. Depending on the respective skills and tactics of the competitors, a competition between mushrooms may result in a variety of outcomes, including domination, cohabitation, or exclusion.

- Predation is the connection and interaction between two species in which the predator kills and eats the prey in order to get nutrients and energy. When mushrooms come into contact with and feed on other fungus or other species in the environment, such as bacteria, nematodes, or insects, they are considered predators. Depending on the relative number and significance of the predators and prey, predator-prey relationships may lead to trophic transfer, biodiversity preservation, or population control, among other outcomes.

- Mutualism is the term for an interaction and connection in which two or more organisms gain from one another and contribute to one another's survival and development.

When mushrooms interact and work together with other fungus or other species in the environment, including plants, animals, or microbes, this is known as mutualism. They trade advantages like nutrition, defense, or dispersion with their mates. Mushroom mutualism contributes to the stability and variety of the environment by promoting the development and survival of both partners. The following are a few typical forms of mutualism that affect mushrooms:

- Lichen: A mutualistic partnership in which a fungus supplies the photosynthetic partner with organic carbon from photosynthesis while the partner provides the fungus with support and protection. Examples of these partners include algae and cyanobacteria. In the ecosystem, lichen is a special and varied collection of organisms that can colonize and survive in hard and severe conditions like rocks, bark, or dirt.

- A mutualistic association known as "mycorrhiza" occurs when a fungus and a plant's roots work together to help the plant collect nutrients and water from the soil, and the plant gives the fungus organic carbon from photosynthesis. Mycorrhiza is widely distributed and vital to the health and development of the majority of plants in the environment, particularly trees.

- Endophyte: A mutualistic relationship in which a fungus lives inside a plant without harming it and benefits the plant in a variety of ways, such as increased resistance to pathogens, pests, drought, or salinity. This relationship can occur in the leaves, stems, or seeds of the plant. Endophyte is a frequent and pervasive phenomenon that has an impact on the ecology and physiology of many different plants in the environment, particularly grasses.

- There are many more forms of mutualism utilizing mushrooms to learn about and investigate; these are only a few examples. A interesting and significant part of mushroom ecology is mutualism, which demonstrates how mushrooms may work together and live with other creatures in the environment.

The ecological threats and challenges of mushrooms

The habitat that mushrooms live in is full of natural and man-made hazards and difficulties that may compromise their variety, survival, and ability to perform their intended functions. Among the risks and difficulties that mushrooms pose to the environment are:

- Loss and fragmentation of habitat: For development and reproduction, mushrooms need certain substrates and ecosystems, such as ponds, grasslands, and woods. However, due to human activities like mining, deforestation, agriculture, and urbanization, many of these habitats and substrates are being destroyed or degraded. Loss and fragmentation of habitat may isolate or eradicate mushroom populations and communities, as well as lower the quantity and quality of nutrients available to mushrooms.

- Climate change: The growth, development, and dispersion of mushrooms may be impacted by variations in temperature, moisture content, and seasonality. The environmental patterns and circumstances to which mushrooms are acclimated may change due to climate change, posing new risks and difficulties for them. For instance, changes in climate may result in more frequent and intense storms, fires, floods, or droughts, which may harm or completely destroy the substrates and habitats of mushrooms. In addition to altering the phenological cycles and geographic ranges of mushrooms and the creatures they are connected with, climate change has the potential to disturb the linkages and ecological interactions among mushrooms.

- Pollution and contamination: The environment around mushrooms exposes them to a variety of pollutants and toxins, including pesticides, herbicides, fertilizers, heavy metals, and radioactive materials. The physiology and metabolism of the mushrooms may be impacted by the buildup of these toxins and pollutants in their tissues. The chemical and biological characteristics of mushroom habitats and substrates, as well as the quantity and quality of nutrients and water, may all be changed by pollution and contamination. In addition to endangering the health and production of mushrooms, pollution and contamination may also affect the species that eat them, including people.

- Overharvesting and exploitation: Mushrooms are an important and sought-after resource for a variety of applications, including biotechnology, medicine, and food. But for economic or recreational purposes, people overharvest and abuse some mushrooms. The capacity for mushroom reproduction and spread may be hampered by overharvesting and exploitation, which can also reduce the genetic variety and natural populations of the species. In addition to disrupting or damaging mushroom habitats and substrates, overharvesting and exploitation may also have an impact on the ecological roles and functions of mushrooms.

- Exotic and invasive species: A variety of ecological creatures, including bacteria, plants, animals, and other fungi, compete with and prey on mushrooms. Nonetheless, a portion of these species are alien and invasive, having been brought about by human activity, whether on purpose or accidentally. It is possible for foreign and invasive species to parasitize, outcompete, or feed on mushrooms, which lowers their variety and abundance. The structure, functionality, and ecological linkages of mushroom habitats and substrates may all be impacted by invasive and alien species.

The ecological benefits and opportunities of mushrooms

Through their interactions with other animals and the environment, mushrooms provide a variety of direct and indirect advantages and possibilities to the ecosystem. The following are a few advantages and chances mushrooms provide for ecology:

- Decomposition and nutrient cycling: In the environment, mushrooms are the main organisms that break down organic materials, such as wood, leaves, and animal corpses. They release digestive enzymes into the substrate, which reduce the substrate's complex organic compounds to simpler forms that the hyphae can ingest. After being ingested, the molecules are either utilized to create new fungal biomass or to provide energy for the fungus to grow and reproduce. Mushroom decomposition contributes to the ecosystem's ability to recycle carbon and nutrients and to keep the carbon and nutrient cycles intact.

- Mutualism and symbiosis: In the environment, mushrooms are involved in several symbiotic and mutualistic partnerships with other creatures, including plants, animals, and other fungus. Benefits like nutrition, water, shelter, or dispersion are traded with their partners. Mushroom symbiosis and mutualism contribute to the stability and variety of the environment by promoting the development and survival of both partners. Among the frequent forms of mutualism and symbiosis involving mushrooms are:
  - A symbiotic and mutualistic interaction known as "mycorrhiza" occurs when a fungus and a plant work together to help the plant collect nutrients and water from the soil, while the plant gives the fungus organic carbon via photosynthesis. Mycorrhiza is widely distributed and vital to the health and development of the majority of plants in the environment, particularly trees.
  - Lichen: A symbiotic and mutualistic association between a fungus and a photosynthetic partner, such as an alga or cyanobacterium, in which the partner supplies the fungus with organic carbon via

photosynthesis while the fungus offers the partner protection and sustenance. In the ecosystem, lichen is a special and varied collection of organisms that can colonize and survive in hard and severe conditions like rocks, bark, or dirt.

- o An endophyte is a fungus that lives in a plant's tissues, such as its leaves, stems, or seeds, in a symbiotic and mutualistic relationship. The plant gains benefits from the fungus in many ways, including increased resistance to pathogens, pests, drought, or salinity. Endophyte is a frequent and pervasive phenomenon that has an impact on the ecology and physiology of many different plants in the environment, particularly grasses.

- Biocontrol and bioremediation: Using their biological and chemical properties, mushrooms are involved in numerous biocontrol and bioremediation processes within the ecosystem. These processes involve the control or degradation of undesirable or harmful organisms or substances, such as pollutants, weeds, pathogens, pests, or contaminants. By acting as biocontrol and bioremediation agents, mushrooms may lessen the need for and effects of synthetic chemicals like fertilizers, herbicides, and pesticides while also enhancing the ecosystem's overall health and quality. Among the instances of how mushrooms are used for biocontrol and bioremediation are:

- o Mycopesticides are mushrooms that release spores or compounds that may either kill or stop the development of pests in the environment, such as nematodes, mites, and insects. Aphids, whiteflies, and beetles are just a few examples of the many insect pests that the entomopathogenic fungus Beauveria bassiana may infect and eradicate within the environment.

- o Mycoherbicides are fungi or chemicals produced by mushrooms that have the ability to either kill or stop the development of weeds in the environment, including plants, algae, and fungus. Chondrostereum purpureum, for instance, is a parasitic fungus that may infect and destroy a variety of woody weeds in the environment, including poplar, willow, and blackberry.

- o Mycoremediation: The process by which mushrooms generate chemicals or enzymes capable of breaking down or purifying toxins or pollutants found in the environment, such as organic compounds, radioactive materials, and heavy metals. For instance, the white rot fungus

Phanerochaete chrysosporium is capable of breaking down a variety of organic contaminants in the environment, including pesticides, dioxins, and polycyclic aromatic hydrocarbons.

- Biodiversity and ecosystem services: The ecosystem is made up of all the many kinds of life and all the activities that maintain and improve both the environment and human well-being. The sources and indicators of biodiversity and ecosystem services in the ecosystem include mushrooms. The environment's resilience and balance are preserved by the biodiversity and ecological services that mushrooms provide. They also provide several advantages and possibilities for people, including food, medicine, and biotechnology. Here are a few instances of how mushrooms contribute to ecosystem services and biodiversity:
  - Food and nutrition: Packed with different proteins, vitamins, minerals, antioxidants, and other bioactive components, mushrooms are a tasty and healthy food source for both people and animals. In the ecosystem, mushrooms may also be grown or collected from a variety of substrates or habitats, including forests, grasslands, and agricultural wastes.

- Health and medicine: Due to their ability to create a wide range of chemicals or compounds with a variety of pharmacological effects, including antibacterial, antifungal, antiviral, anti-inflammatory, immunomodulatory, and anticancer properties, mushrooms are a powerful and useful source of medication for both people and animals. In the environment, mushrooms may also be used or developed into medications, vitamins, or cosmeceuticals.

- Biotechnology and innovation: Due to their diverse biological and chemical properties, including the ability to produce enzymes, convert biomass, undergo genetic engineering, and engage in biomimicry, mushrooms provide a viable and adaptable biotechnology source for both humans and animals. In the ecosystem, mushrooms may also be used or created as biomaterials, biofuels, biosensors, or bioinspirations.

The life cycle and reproduction of mushrooms

Depending on the kind and species of fungus, mushrooms have a complex and varied life cycle and reproductive system.

Nonetheless, the majority of mushrooms go through a few common phases and procedures that may be summed up as follows:

- **Spore production and dispersal.** At this point in their life cycle, mature mushrooms either release their spores into the air or water or attach them to animals or objects. It is the first and final stage of the mushroom life cycle. The small, unicellular spores are often haploid, or made up of just one pair of chromosomes. Fungi primarily reproduce and spread via their spores, which are susceptible to many environmental elements, including light, moisture, and temperature. As a result, only a few spores will make it and begin to germinate.

- **Spore germination and hyphal growth.** This is the second stage of the mushroom life cycle, during which the spores begin to develop and form hyphae if they fall on an appropriate substrate, such as soil, wood, or organic waste. The hyphae are filamentous, tubular, and often septate, which means that they are divided into segments by cross-walls. In order to grow, the hyphae branch out and extend their tips, creating a network known as the mycelium. The mycelium creates enzymes to disassemble complex organic compounds into simpler ones while absorbing nutrients and water from the substrate.

- **Mycelial fusion and dikaryon formation.** In the third stage of the life cycle of a mushroom, two mycelia belonging to the same species but with distinct mating preferences fuse together to produce a dikaryon. A dikaryon is a kind of mycelium that typically has two sets of chromosomes and has two nuclei per segment—one from each parent. Sexual reproduction produces the dikaryon, which boosts the fungi's genetic variety and adaptability. The dikaryon has a protracted growth and persistence period, until it finds circumstances that allow it to make mushrooms.

- **Fruiting body formation and development.** The dikaryon creates a primordium in this stage of the mushroom life cycle, which is a tiny, spherical, dense clump of hyphae that will eventually become a fruiting body. The structure that holds and distributes the spores is called the fruiting body, often referred to as the sporocarp or the mushroom. The fruiting body may contain a variety of characteristics, including rings, veils, volvas, teeth, gills, pores, and caps and stems, in addition to varying sizes, colors, and forms. Environmental cues that cause the hyphae to differentiate and specialize—such as temperature, moisture, light, or nutrients—lead to the development of the fruiting body.

- **Spore formation and maturation.** In the fifth stage of the life cycle of a mushroom, the spores are produced and matured by the fruiting body. Two nuclei from distinct dikaryon segments fuse to generate spores via a process known as meiosis, which is a kind of cell division that results in a halving of the chromosome count. Spores are often formed on specialized structures on the underside of the cap or on the sides or top of the fruiting body, such as gills, holes, teeth, or tubes. The spore coat, a thick coating that gives the spores their many colors, shapes, and decorations, often protects them.

Chapter 2: How to Identify Mushrooms and Avoid Poisonous Ones

Within the kingdom of fungus, mushrooms are a varied and intriguing collection of creatures. They inhabit a wide range of ecosystems, including grasslands, woodlands, deserts, and even aquatic ones. While some mushrooms are toxic and lethal, others are tasty and edible. As such, it is critical to be able to safely and accurately identify mushrooms and to refrain from eating any that you are unsure about. This chapter will cover the traits and properties of mushrooms as well as the common and scientific names for some of the more common and hazardous varieties.

The characteristics and features of mushrooms

Some fungi create fruiting bodies, or mushrooms, which are the structures that generate and spread spores, which are tiny fungus seeds. The biology of mushrooms is intricate and dynamic, despite their simple and exquisite morphology. In addition to their two primary components, the cap and stem, they may also contain other characteristics like rings, veils, teeth, holes, gills, or bulbs. Mushroom species vary greatly in their form, size, color, texture, and arrangement of these characteristics, all of which may be used to identify and categorize the species.

The top portion of the mushroom that covers and shields the area that produces spores is called the cap, often referred to as the pileus. The cap's surfaces might be smooth, scaly, warty, hairy, or irregular. It can also be flat, convex, conical, bell-shaped, or uneven. Depending on the species and age of the mushroom, the cap may also have distinct colors, patterns, or markings. The cap may be free of the stem or fastened to it via a central, eccentric, or lateral point.

The portion of the mushroom that produces and releases the spores is called the spore-producing surface, or hymenium. The surface of the mushroom that produces spores might be found on the top, sides, or underside of the cap. The surface that produces spores may take on many shapes, including tubes, gills, holes, and teeth. From the stem to the edge of the cap, the gills are thin, plate-like structures. The surface of the mushroom is covered with tiny, angular, or spherical pores. The teeth are lengthy projections that dangle from the mushroom's surface and resemble needles or spines. The tubes are lodged in the mushroom's body and might be hollow, cylindrical, or labyrinthine.

The tiny, unicellular reproductive units of fungus are called spores. Numerous processes, including wind, rain, insects, and animals, release the spores into the air or water when they are created in significant quantities by the spore-producing surface. Based on the species and staining technique, the spores may have a variety of colors, sizes, and ornamentations in addition to their typical spherical, oval, or elliptical form. Additionally, the number of nuclei in the spores may vary, from one (haploid) to four (tetraploid).

The portion of the mushroom that upholds and supports the cap is called the stem, often referred to as the stipe. The stem may vary in length, breadth, form, and texture, and it can be central, eccentric, lateral, or nonexistent. Additionally, the stem may have various characteristics, like a bulb, ring, veil, or volva. The ring, sometimes called the annulus, is a piece of the partial veil, a thin membrane that covers a juvenile mushroom's pores or gills. The ring may have many locations, forms, and textures in addition to being either permanent, transient, or nonexistent. Young mushrooms have a veil, sometimes called a cortina, which is a web-like or cobwebby tissue that joins the cap and stem. A partial veil would just cover the pores or gills, but a global veil would cover the whole fruiting body. The veil may have various colors, patterns, or consistencies and can be either permanent, ephemeral, or nonexistent. The volva, often referred to as the cup, is a piece of the thick membrane that surrounds the whole fruiting body of young mushrooms, known as the universal veil. The volva comes in a variety of sizes, forms, and textures and might resemble a bag, cup, or collar. The bulb, often referred to as the basal bulb, is an inflated or swollen base of the stem that may be indicative of a volva.

The portion of the mushroom that fills the cap and stem is called the flesh, or context. The species and age of the mushroom may affect the flesh's colors, textures, tastes, scents, and responses. Additionally, the flesh may have layers such as the medulla, cuticle, pileipellis, or trama. The outermost layer of the cap is called the cuticle, or pellicle, and may be hairy, scaly, smooth, or warty. The layer of tissue covering the cuticle, which may be cellular, filamentous, or gelatinous, is called the pileipellis, or cap skin. The primary tissue that fills the cap and stem is called the trama, or flesh proper. It may be homogenous, heterogeneous, or zonate. The center of the stem, often referred to as the medulla, may be packed, hollow, or solid.

The common and scientific names of mushrooms

Every species of mushroom has a distinct scientific name that is used by scientists to identify and categorize it. The genus and the species are the two components that normally make up a scientific name. Agaricus bisporus, for instance, is the scientific name for the white button mushroom. The group to which the fungus belongs is called Agaricus, and the particular species within that group is called bisporus. The initial letter of the genus is capitalized, the first letter of the species is lowercase, and the scientific name is often written in italics. The name of the taxonomic rank under the species, such as the variation or subspecies, or the name of the person who wrote the first description of the mushroom may sometimes be included in the scientific name.

In addition, non-scientists often refer to mushrooms by their common names, which differ based on the locale and cultural context. Because several mushrooms may have the same common name or multiple popular names for the same mushroom, common names may be less accurate than scientific names. For instance, the oyster mushroom, scientifically known as Pleurotus ostreatus, is a popular term for a variety of distinct types of mushrooms. Agaricus campestris, the scientific name for what is usually termed the field or meadow mushroom, is also often referred to as the pink bottom, champignon, or Scotch bonnet.

The following is a list of some of the most well-known and hazardous mushrooms, along with their common and scientific names:

- **Portobello mushroom**: Agaricus bisporus. One of the most extensively grown and eaten mushrooms in the world is this one. It features a broad white stem and a huge brown umbrella-shaped top. It has a moderate, nutty taste and may be eaten raw or cooked. It goes by many other names, including baby bella, button mushroom, cremini, and common store mushroom.

Portobello mushroom

- **Shiitake mushroom**: Lentinula edodes. In Asia, this is one of the most well-liked and nutrient-dense mushrooms. It features a cream-colored stem and a brown, convex top. It has a deep, smokey taste and may be consumed fresh or dried. It goes by many other names, including Chinese black mushroom, golden oak mushroom, and black forest mushroom.

Shiitake mushroom

- **Chanterelle mushroom**: Cantharellus cibarius. One of the most valuable and sought-after mushrooms on the planet is this one. It features a smooth golden stem and a yellow funnel-shaped top. It has a delicious, spicy taste and may be consumed fresh or dried. It is also referred to as the girolle, the egg mushroom, or the golden chanterelle.

Chanterelle mushroom

- **Morel mushroom**: Morchella spp. One of the world's most unique and tasty mushrooms is this one. It features a hollow, white stem and a brown, conical, honeycombed top. It tastes earthy and nutty and may be eaten either fresh or dry. It goes by the names sponge, pinecone, and brain mushroom as well.

Morel mushroom

- **Death cap mushroom**: Amanita phalloides. This is among the world's deadliest and most toxic mushrooms. It has a white stem with a ring and a volva, as well as a greenish-white, convex cap. Although it is readily confused for an edible fungus, it contains toxins that may lead to fatal liver failure. It is sometimes referred to as the green death cap, the destroying angel, or the death angel.

Death cap mushroom

- **Fly agaric mushroom**: Amanita muscaria. One of the most well-known and hallucinogenic mushrooms on the planet is this one. It features a white stem with a ring and a volva, and a brilliant red, convex crown with white dots. It is used as a recreational drug and as a religious sacrament, although it may also result in hallucinations, delirium, and nausea. It goes by many other names, including red cap, toadstool, and fairy tale mushroom.

Fly agaric mushroom

- **Lion's mane mushroom**: Hericium erinaceus. Among the world's most unusual and therapeutic mushrooms is this one

Lion's mane mushroom

Its fruiting body is white, globular, or icicle-shaped, and coated in long, soft spines. It tastes like fish and may be consumed either fresh or dry. It is also well recognized for its nerve-regenerating, cognitive-improving, and neuroprotective qualities. It is often referred to as the hedgehog mushroom, the bearded tooth mushroom, or the pom pom mushroom.

- **Porcini mushroom**: Boletus edulis. One of the world's most costly and delectable mushrooms is this one. It features a thick, white stem with holes in place of gills and a brown, convex cap. It tastes meaty and nutty and may be eaten fresh or dry. It has high levels of fiber, protein, and antioxidants. It goes by other names, such as the penny bun, the cep, and the king bolete.

Porcini mushroom

- **Truffle mushroom**: Tuber spp. One of the rarest and most expensive mushrooms on the planet is this one. It is a kind of underground fungus that coexists with certain trees, such as pine, oak, and hazel. It is colored black, brown, white, or gray, and it has a rounded, uneven, or lobed form. It smells strong, earthy, or garlicky, and it may be eaten fresh or preserved. It is an aphrodisiac and a delicacy as well. It goes by the names desert truffle, white gold, and black diamond as well.

Truffle mushroom

The edible and poisonous mushrooms and their look-alikes

Though hundreds of species exist worldwide, only a few are thought to be edible. There are edible mushrooms that are more prevalent and well-liked than others, and others have readily mistaken them for dangerous lookalikes. Here are some illustrations of both toxic and edible mushrooms, along with information on how to distinguish between the two:

- **Morel mushroom**: Morchella spp. One of the world's most unique and tasty mushrooms is this one. It features a hollow, white stem and a brown, conical, honeycombed top. It tastes earthy and nutty and may be eaten either fresh or dry. It goes by the names sponge, pinecone, and brain mushroom as well.

- **False morel mushroom**: Gyromitra spp. This is among the world's deadliest and most toxic mushrooms. It features a pure white stem and a dark, uneven top that resembles a brain. It may result in fatalities, serious gastrointestinal problems, and liver damage. It goes by many other names, such as the elephant ear mushroom, the turban, and the beefsteak.

- **How to tell them apart**: Whereas the fake morel has a cap shaped like a brain connected to the stem at the top, the real morel has a honeycombed cap attached to the stem at the base. The stem of a fake morel is solid, while that of a real morel is hollow. The scent of a real morel is pleasant, whereas that of a counterfeit morel is unpleasant.

- **Chanterelle mushroom**: Cantharellus cibarius. One of the most valuable and sought-after mushrooms on the planet is this one. It features a smooth golden stem and a yellow funnel-shaped top. It has a delicious, spicy taste and may be consumed fresh or dried. It is also referred to as the girolle, the egg mushroom, or the golden chanterelle.

- **Jack-o'-lantern mushroom**: Omphalotus spp. Among the most prevalent and deadly mushrooms worldwide is this one. It has a white stem with a ring and a volva, as well as an orange, convex cap. It may result in cramping, diarrhea, and vomiting. It is sometimes referred to as the ghost fungus, the foxfire mushroom, or the false chanterelle.

- **How to tell them apart**:

- While the jack-o'-lantern has actual gills that end at the stem, the chanterelle has ridges that resemble gills that go down the stem. The spore print on the chanterelle is white, but the spore print on the jack-o'-lantern is cream. The chanterelle has a delightful aroma, but the jack-o'-lantern has a subtle or disagreeable scent.

- **Oyster mushroom**: Pleurotus ostreatus. Among the world's most well-liked and nutrient-dense mushrooms is this one. It features a short lateral stem and a fan-shaped head that may be white, gray, or brown. It has a delicate taste akin to shellfish and may be eaten either fresh or dried. It is sometimes referred to as the abalone mushroom, tree oyster, or pearl oyster.

- **Angel's wing mushroom**: Pleurocybella porrigens. This is among the rarest and deadliest mushrooms on the planet. It has a short lateral stem and a white, fan-shaped crown. It may result in death and brain damage. It is sometimes referred to as the angel's wing mushroom, white oyster, or sugihiratake.

- **How to tell them apart**:

- The cap of an oyster mushroom is thick and meaty, while the cap of an angel's wing mushroom is thin and papery. The edge of an oyster mushroom is level and smooth, whereas the margin of an angel's wing mushroom is uneven and wavy. The spore print of an oyster mushroom is lilac, while that of an angel's wing mushroom is white.

The rules and tips for mushroom identification

Identification of mushrooms is a skill that has to be practiced carefully and methodically, particularly if you want to consume them. The age, stage, environment, and damage of mushrooms are only a few of the many variables that may alter their look and features. Therefore, thorough observation and evaluation of many attributes is more important than relying just on images or superficial aspects. The following guidelines and pointers may help you identify mushrooms:

- **Rule: Don't consume a mushroom until you are certain of its identity.** The most crucial and fundamental guideline for mushroom foraging is this one. Many lethal and toxic mushrooms may have edible appearances, and vice versa. Make sure you confirm and cross-reference your findings with credible sources, even if you believe you have discovered a common or well-known mushroom. Do not consume it if you are unsure or doubtful about something. Being safe is preferable to being sorry.

- **Rule: Acquire knowledge of the traits and attributes of mushrooms.** The biology of mushrooms is intricate and dynamic, despite their simple and exquisite morphology. In addition to their two primary components, the cap and stem, they may also contain other characteristics like rings, veils, teeth, holes, gills, or bulbs. Mushroom species vary greatly in their form, size, color, texture, and arrangement of these characteristics, all of which may be used to identify and categorize the species. Discover how to recognize and characterize these characteristics, as well as how to use them to differentiate between various mushroom species and groupings.

- **Rule: Acquire knowledge of the scientific and colloquial names of mushrooms.** Every species of mushroom has a distinct scientific name that is used by scientists to identify and categorize it. The genus and the species are the two components that normally make up a scientific name. Agaricus bisporus, for instance, is the scientific name for the white button mushroom. The group to which the fungus belongs is called Agaricus, and the particular species within that group is called bisporus. The initial letter of the genus is capitalized, the first letter of the species is lowercase, and the scientific name is often written in italics. The name of the taxonomic rank under the species, such as the variation or subspecies, or the name of the person who wrote the first description of the mushroom may sometimes be included in the scientific name. In addition, non-scientists often refer to mushrooms by their common names, which differ based on the locale and cultural context. Because several mushrooms may have the same common name or multiple popular names for the same mushroom, common names may be less accurate than scientific names. For instance, the oyster mushroom, scientifically known as Pleurotus ostreatus, is a popular term for a variety of distinct types of mushrooms. Agaricus campestris, the scientific name for what is usually termed the field or meadow mushroom, is also often referred to as the pink bottom, champignon, or Scotch bonnet. Acquire knowledge of the common and scientific names of the mushrooms you come across, and use them to cross-reference and authenticate data from other sources.

- **Rule: Acquire knowledge about the mushroom's habitat and season.** There are many different types of habitats for mushrooms, including grasslands, woods, deserts, and even aquatic ones. They may grow on a variety of surfaces, including wood, soil, and organic materials. Additionally, they may play a variety of ecological functions, such as that of mycorrhizal organisms, which create symbiotic connections with plants, saprotrophs, which feed on dead or decaying materials, and parasitic creatures, which infect and injure other living things. Moreover, the season in which mushrooms fruit varies based on the species and region. Certain mushrooms bear fruit in the spring, while others do so in the summer, autumn, or winter. While some mushrooms only bear fruit once a year, others do so several times. Discover the habitat and season of the mushrooms you come across, and make use of this information to focus your search and confirm the identification.

- **Rule: Acquire knowledge of mushroom chemical reactions and spore prints.** The pattern of spores that a mushroom leaves on a material, such as foil, glass, or paper, is called a spore print. The color, shape, size, and ornamentation of the spores—all crucial characteristics for identification and classification—can be seen in the spore print. Spore prints with similar characteristics but distinct spore colors may also be distinguished from one another using the spore print. Cut off the stem of a fresh mushroom, set the cap gill-side down on a surface, cover it with a bowl or a glass, and let it sit for a few hours or overnight in order to create a spore print. Spores will drop from the pores or gills and leave a surface imprint. A variety of hues, including white, cream, yellow, pink, brown, purple, black, or green, may be seen in the spore print.

- The color, smell, and taste changes that mushrooms experience in response to certain substances—like phenol, potassium hydroxide, ammonia, iron salts, and iodine—are known as chemical reactions. Certain chemicals or colors that are important for identification and classification might be revealed by the chemical processes inside the mushroom. Additionally, the chemical reactions may be used to distinguish between lookalikes with differing chemical responses but comparable characteristics. Applying a drop or smear of the material to a fresh or dried portion of the mushroom, such as the cap, stem, gills, or meat, and watching the response is how you accomplish a chemical reaction. Various outcomes are possible from the response, including no change, color, odor, or taste changes.

- There are several guidelines and pointers for identifying mushrooms; these are only a few of them. Practice and knowledge are required. Before eating any mushrooms, always remember to identify them carefully and methodically and to check with a variety of sources, such as field guides, internet sites, and knowledgeable mushroom aficionados.

The common mushroom poisoning symptoms and treatments

Eating poisonous mushrooms may result in mycetism, or mushroom poisoning, which is a deadly and sometimes fatal condition. There are many kinds of mushrooms that are hazardous to people; they include alkaloids, peptides, and glycoproteins that are harmful to different bodily organs and systems. The kind and quantity of mushrooms consumed, the time of consumption, the patient's age and condition, and the accessibility of medical care are all factors that affect the symptoms and management of mushroom poisoning.

Early-onset (within hours) mushrooms are often less harmful than late-onset (typically beyond hours) mushrooms. Early signs and symptoms are often gastrointestinal in nature, including cramps, nausea, vomiting, diarrhea, and stomach discomfort. Muscarine-containing mushrooms, such as Inocybe and some Clitocybe species, or irritant-containing mushrooms, like Chlorophyllum molybdites, are the source of these symptoms. Symptomatic and supportive measures, such as electrolyte and fluid replacement, antiemetics, and antispasmodics, are often used to treat these instances. Severe muscarinic symptoms, including lacrimation, increased salivation, sweating, and bronchospasm, may be treated with atropine.

Hemolysis, coagulopathy, central nervous system depression, liver failure, renal failure, and other serious, systemic symptoms are often the later ones. Mushrooms that contain gyromitrin, like Gyromitra esculenta and similar species, or amatoxins, like

Amanita phalloides and related species, are the source of these symptoms. More severe and targeted treatments, such as gastric lavage, activated charcoal, penicillin, silibinin, thioctic acid, N-acetylcysteine, hemodialysis, or liver transplantation, are used for these situations.

Psychoactive effects, including anxiety, paranoia, euphoria, hallucinations, and altered perception, may also be caused by certain mushrooms. Mushrooms containing psilocybin, like Psilocybe and similar species, or ibotenic acid and muscimol, like Amanita muscaria and related species, are responsible for these effects. Since the symptoms in these situations are often transient and not life-threatening, the conventional course of therapy is monitoring, sedation, and reassurance.

The most crucial step in treating mushroom poisoning is to identify the species of mushroom that is causing it, if at all feasible. To do this, bring a sample of the mushroom or a picture of it to the poison control center or your healthcare professional. This may assist in identifying the kind and intensity of the poisoning and in selecting the best course of action. However, since many mushrooms have changeable traits or similar appearances, mushroom identification may be challenging and inaccurate, particularly for beginners. Thus, the greatest defense against mushroom poisoning is to abstain from consuming any wild mushrooms that have not been conclusively determined to be edible by a qualified authority.

The legal and regulatory issues related to mushroom foraging

Foraging for mushrooms, or gathering wild mushrooms for one's own or another's use, is a common and fulfilling hobby for many. However, since certain regions may have limitations or bans to safeguard the environment, public health, or property rights, mushroom foragers should also be aware of the legal and regulatory problems surrounding mushroom foraging.

Foraging for mushrooms raises different legal and regulatory challenges in different nations, states, and localities that might evolve over time. Consequently, before mushroom foraging in any location, foragers should always confirm that the laws and regulations in effect are up-to-date and adhere to any applicable standards. The following are a few typical legal and regulatory concerns pertaining to mushroom foraging:

- Permits and harvesting: Certain regions may restrict the quantity, species, or site of mushroom harvesting, and may require foragers to get permission or a license before harvesting mushrooms for personal or commercial use. For instance, in the US, mushroom harvesting on federal lands is governed by the Forest Service of the U.S. Department of Agriculture, and anybody planning to sell mushrooms must get commercial permission. The harvest season, harvest quota, harvest area, and harvest charge may all be specified in the permit. The legal limit for personal consumption is usually one gallon of any one variety of mushrooms per day. On state or private property, mushroom harvesting may be subject to various laws and ordinances in different states and towns, and some may outright forbid it. As a result, before gathering mushrooms in any location, mushroom foragers should always confirm with the appropriate authorities and show respect for the landowners' private property rights.

- Identification and certification: In some regions, in order to utilize mushrooms for personal or commercial purposes, mushroom foragers may need to prove their expertise in the identification of mushrooms. They may also need to receive registration or certification from an established body or institution. For instance, the Food and Drug Administration (FDA) in the US controls the retail sale and handling of wild mushrooms and mandates that the mushrooms be recognized and deemed safe by a designated expert in mushroom identification. Together with the FDA

Food Code, which identifies select wild mushroom species with culinary value and their corresponding identification requirements, the FDA also offers model guidelines that state, municipal, and tribal regulatory bodies may use. However, laws governing the identification and certification of mushrooms may vary throughout states and locales, with some imposing stricter or more particular standards than others. As a result, before offering or selling wild mushrooms in any location, mushroom gatherers should always confirm the mushrooms' safety and quality with the appropriate authorities.

- Sustainability and conservation: To preserve the natural ecosystem and the biodiversity of the mushrooms, some places may implement sustainability and conservation measures. These measures may limit or control the equipment used for collecting, the techniques used, or the effects of mushroom foragers' gathering activities. For instance, the Wildlife and Countryside Act in the United Kingdom forbids the purposeful gathering, uprooting, or destruction of any wild plant, including mushrooms, without the owner's or occupier's consent. The Act also forbids the marketing or selling of any wild plant that has been illegally harvested, including mushrooms. However, laws and policies pertaining to the sustainability and conservation of mushrooms may vary throughout nations and areas, and some may have more stringent or all-encompassing policies. Consequently, before harvesting mushrooms in any area, mushroom foragers should always confirm with the appropriate authorities. They should also adhere to the best practices for mushroom conservation and sustainability, which include harvesting only a portion of what they find, avoiding damaging the mycelium—the vegetative part of a mushroom—and protecting wildlife habitats.

Foraging for mushrooms may be an enjoyable and fulfilling hobby, but it also has certain hazards and obligations. In addition to always being mindful and responsible while foraging in any location, mushroom gatherers should use extreme caution when gathering, identifying, and ingesting wild mushrooms. In addition, mushroom foragers need to be aware of the legal and regulatory ramifications associated with their activities and ensure that they always abide by any laws and regulations. By doing this, mushroom foragers may safeguard the environment and the general public's health while also taking delight in the advantages and joys of mushroom foraging.

Chapter 3: How to Harvest, Store, and Preserve Mushrooms

Fly agaric mushroom

You can cultivate mushrooms at home or find them in the wild; they are really tasty and nourishing delicacies. To guarantee their quality and safety, mushrooms must be harvested, stored, and preserved, which calls for considerable knowledge and expertise. Some of the fundamentals of mushroom foraging will be covered in this chapter, including where and when to hunt for mushrooms, how to recognize and steer clear of hazardous ones, and how to harvest and handle them safely. We will also go over some of the processes and procedures for canning, pickling, drying, freezing, and storing mushrooms.

The best time and place to find mushrooms

Fungi are creatures that break down organic debris and recycle nutrients in the environment. Their fruiting bodies are mushrooms. Hyphae, which are tiny threads that create a network known as a mycelium, are the means by which fungi grow. Usually concealed beneath or within wood, the mycelium develops mushrooms to spread spores and reproduce when the right circumstances are met, including light, moisture, and temperature.

The season and weather have an impact on the optimal time to discover mushrooms. In general, when the weather is moderate and there is a lot of rainfall, mushrooms grow more prolifically in the spring and autumn. Nevertheless, depending on the species and the environment, some mushrooms may grow in either the summer or the winter. For instance, oysters are a common and adaptable fungus that may grow year-round, whereas morels, which are highly valued culinary mushrooms, often emerge in the spring.

The substrate and environment determine where to locate mushrooms the best. Different types of mushrooms have preferred environments, including fields, lawns, woodlands, and meadows. Certain varieties of mushrooms grow on or on the roots, trunks, or branches of trees that are associated with them, such as pine, oak, or birch. Certain mushrooms may be found growing on rotting or dead wood, such as twigs, stumps, or logs. Certain mushrooms may be found growing on grass, moss, dirt, or leaf litter. Certain mushrooms may be grown in mulch, compost, or animal manure.

You must search the ground, the trees, and the plants very carefully and meticulously in order to discover mushrooms. To make the mushrooms visible, you may need to push away some grass, leaves, or branches. For some mushrooms that are concealed or just partly buried, you may additionally need to use a knife, a shovel, or a stick. In order to inspect certain mushrooms that are tiny, dark, or difficult to see, you may also need to use a magnifying glass, a flashlight, or a mirror.

Common and edible mushrooms that grow wild include the following:

- Morels: These are brown, yellow, or black mushrooms in cone form with a texture like honeycomb. They often grow in hardwood woods in the spring, particularly close to apple, ash, and dead or dying elm trees. They are quite popular among mushroom enthusiasts and have an earthy, nutty taste.
- Chanterelles: These are trumpet-shaped mushrooms that are yellow, orange, or white in color, with a smooth or wavy crown. They often grow in mixed or coniferous woods in

the summer and autumn, particularly next to oak, birch, or pine trees. They are often used in gourmet cooking and have a fruity and spicy taste.

- **Boletes-Mushroom**

Boletes Mushroom

These mushrooms have a cap and a stem, but underneath the cap are tubes or pores that serve as gills. They grow throughout the summer and autumn, mainly in woods or grasslands, often next to trees or bushes, and vary in a variety of sizes, forms, and colors. They are popular in soups, stews, and sauces and have a savory, meaty taste.

- Oysters Mushroom:

- These mushrooms have a small stem or none at all, with a cap that resembles an oyster or fan. They grow all year on

95

dead or decaying wood, such as logs, stumps, or branches, and occur in a variety of hues, including white, gray, brown, or pink. They may be fried, baked, grilled, or roasted, and their mild and nutty taste makes them a versatile culinary ingredient.

Oysters Mushroom

- Shiitake mushrooms have a robust, woody stem and a convex or umbrella-shaped cap. Their surface is broken or scaly, and they are colored black or brown. They often grow on hardwood logs like oak, beech, or maple throughout the summer and autumn. Their umami and smokey taste make them a popular ingredient in Asian dishes such as stir-fries, soups, and noodles.

The proper way to collect and handle mushrooms

Once you've located any mushrooms you wish to harvest, you must gather and treat them carefully to guarantee their safety and quality. Here are some pointers and recommendations for managing and gathering mushrooms:

- Employ the proper equipment: To remove the mushrooms from their substrate, you'll need a sharp knife, a trowel, or scissors. You'll also need a basket, a cloth bag, or a cardboard box to transport them. The mushrooms may deteriorate more quickly if you use a plastic bag since it will retain heat and moisture. A brush, paper towel, or moist cloth could also be necessary to remove any dirt or debris from the mushrooms.

- Harvest carefully: Only mushrooms that are in excellent condition, show no symptoms of rot, damage, or insect infestation, and those you can be certain are edible should be harvested. In order to give the mushrooms time to develop and proliferate, you should also leave some of them, particularly the smaller or younger ones. In addition, you should abide by any laws or ordinances that pertain to the gathering of mushrooms in the region, as well as respect the environment and the landowners' property rights.

- Harvesting mushrooms requires caution. In order to protect the mycelium—the component of the fungus that grows the mushrooms—you should cut them at the base of the stem or just below the soil's or wood's surface. Additionally, you should refrain from tugging or twisting the mushrooms since this might shatter or damage them. Additionally, you want to handle the mushrooms carefully—don't squeeze or crush them. Additionally, you should avoid combining the mushrooms with other plants or materials and instead keep them divided by species.

- Harvest immediately: Depending on the weather and the animals, the mushrooms may decay or perish rapidly, so you should harvest them as soon as possible when they emerge. Additionally, after gathering the mushrooms, you should process them as quickly as possible, since if you wait too long, they may deteriorate or lose their taste and texture. Additionally, you should eat or preserve the mushrooms within a few days after storing them in a cold, dry location.

The methods and techniques to store and preserve mushrooms

Depending on the kind, number, and intended use of the mushrooms, there are many ways to store and preserve them. Several typical approaches and strategies include:

- Cleaning: To get rid of any dirt, debris, or insects that could be clinging to mushrooms, cleaning is a crucial step. However, as mushrooms are sensitive and readily absorb water, cleaning them should be done with caution and gentleness. Using a moist cloth, paper towel, or soft brush to wipe off mushrooms is the best method for cleaning them. As an alternative, you may give them a quick rinse under cold running water; just don't soak or scrub them too hard. Use a paper towel or rag to pat them dry after washing.

- Drying: Since it eliminates the moisture that leads to deterioration and decay, drying mushrooms is an easy and efficient method of preserving them for an extended period of time. In addition to making mushrooms lighter and simpler to store, drying them intensifies their taste and scent. A dehydrator, the sun, an oven, or a microwave are a few methods for drying mushrooms. The fundamental procedure is to lay the thinly sliced mushrooms on a tray or rack, thinly slice them equally, and then expose them to air and heat until they become crisp and brittle. Generally, drying takes a few hours to several days, while the temperature and duration may change based on the kind of mushrooms and the technique used.

- Freezing: As freezing inhibits the enzymatic and microbiological processes that lead to degradation and spoilage, freezing mushrooms is an additional method of long-term preservation. Additionally, compared to other procedures, freezing preserves the color, texture, and nutrition of mushrooms. It is necessary to prepare mushrooms beforehand for freezing, such as by blanching, steaming, or frying them. This is because the enzymes in uncooked mushrooms may induce browning, softness, and taste loss in frozen mushrooms. The fundamental procedures are to slice and clean the mushrooms, cook them for a short while in oil, steam, or boiling water, then immediately chill them in cold water, drain thoroughly, and store them in freezer bags or airtight containers. Depending on the kind and number of mushrooms, the freezing period may vary, but in general, it may last anywhere from a few months to a year.

- Canning: Canning is the process of preserving mushrooms at high pressure and temperature in a liquid solution, such as water, vinegar, or brine. When mushrooms are canned, any potentially dangerous germs are eliminated, and the jars are sealed to keep out moisture and air. In addition to improving their taste and texture, canning mushrooms prepares them for use in a variety of recipes. But canning mushrooms calls for certain tools, such as jars, lids, rings, and pressure canners, as well as safety measures, like using the right processing time and pressure and inspecting the mushrooms' quality and seals before eating. Cleaning, slicing, packing in sterile jars, adding liquid medium and spices, sealing the jars, processing in a pressure canner, cooling, and storing in a cold, dark area are the main stages involved in canning mushrooms. Depending on the size and variety of mushrooms, the canning time and pressure may vary, but generally speaking, it takes minutes at pounds of pressure.

- Pickling: A vinegar solution is used to preserve mushrooms by lowering their pH and preventing the development of germs and fungus. In addition to giving mushrooms a crisp texture and an acidic, spicy taste, pickling them also makes them a good choice for salads, sandwiches, or snacks. But pickled mushrooms call for only a few ingredients—

vinegar, sugar, salt, spices, and herbs—as well as some time—the mushrooms must marinade in the vinegar solution for a few days to a few weeks. Cleaning, slicing, boiling in water for a few minutes, draining, packing in sterilized jars, adding the vinegar solution and spices, sealing the jars, and storing them in the refrigerator or a cold, dark area are the fundamental processes.

The shelf life and quality of mushrooms

A number of variables, including the kind, state, and how the mushrooms are stored, affect the shelf life and quality of mushrooms. A variety of factors, including water content, texture, taste, and scent, influence the shelf life and quality of various kinds of mushrooms. The freshness, maturity, and cleanliness of the mushrooms at the moment of purchase or harvest have an impact on their shelf life and overall quality. The quality and shelf life of the mushrooms are also influenced by the storage conditions, including air movement, humidity, and temperature.

Fresh mushrooms are very perishable and prone to deterioration and decomposition, therefore, their shelf life is usually rather limited. In the refrigerator, fresh mushrooms may keep for a few days, however, this will depend on the kind and state of the mushrooms. For instance, whole mushrooms keep longer than sliced mushrooms, while button and cremini mushrooms keep longer than shiitake and oyster mushrooms. For extended storage, fresh mushrooms may also be frozen, however, this may change the taste and texture of the food.

Because boiling destroys some of the bacteria and enzymes that lead to degradation and spoilage, cooked mushrooms have a somewhat longer shelf life than fresh mushrooms. In the refrigerator, cooked mushrooms may keep for a few hours to several days, however, this will depend on the kind and technique of cooking. For instance, plain mushrooms keep better than seasoned and sauced mushrooms, while boiling and steamed mushrooms stay longer than fried and grilled mushrooms. For extended storage, cooked mushrooms may also be frozen, however, doing so may change the taste and texture of the food.

Since drying eliminates the majority of the moisture that leads to deterioration and decay, dried mushrooms have a much longer shelf life than fresh or cooked mushrooms. Depending on what kind and how they are dried, dried mushrooms may keep for months or even longer. For instance, mushrooms that have been sun-dried, oven-dried, dehydrator-dried, or microwave-dried often have longer shelf lives than mushrooms that have been sliced. To preserve the quality of dried mushrooms, keep them in sealed containers in a cool, dark area away from light and moisture.

Because they are preserved in a liquid medium at high pressure and temperature during the canning process, mushrooms have an extremely extended shelf life. Depending on the manufacturer's recommended expiration date, canned mushrooms may be stored for a year or even longer. Canned mushrooms, however, should be used within a few days after being opened due to their susceptibility to infection and deterioration. Heat and light should not be allowed to degrade the quality of canned mushrooms; instead, they should be kept cold and dark.

Because pickling preserves mushrooms in a vinegar solution that lowers pH and prevents the development of bacteria and fungus, pickled mushrooms have a moderate shelf life. In the refrigerator, pickled mushrooms may keep for many weeks or months; however, this might vary depending on the kind and process used. For instance, pickled mushrooms that are hot-packed and pressure-canning keep longer than those that are cold-packed and water-bath-canning, and entire mushrooms keep longer than slices. To keep the quality of pickled mushrooms unaffected by heat and light, store them somewhere cold and dark.

Mushrooms may be judged for quality based on their texture, flavor, aroma, and appearance. Among the telltale symptoms of high-quality mushrooms are:

- They are plump and solid, not shriveled or slimy.
- Their surface is unbroken and smooth; it isn't fractured or damaged.
- They are neither speckled nor discolored; instead, their color is consistent and natural.
- Rather than being musty or sour, they smell earthy and fresh.
- They taste nutty and mild, neither metallic nor unpleasant.
- Instead of being hard or rubbery, their texture is soft and meaty.

Among the telltale symptoms of poor quality mushrooms are:

- Instead of crisp and crispy, they are mushy and squishy.
- Instead of being dry and smooth, their surface is slimy and sticky.
- Instead of being vivid and dazzling, their hue is dark and muted.
- Instead of being fragrant or pleasant to smell, they smell nasty and awful.
- Rather than being flavorful and delectable, they taste ruined and putrid.
- Instead of being luscious and delicious, they are fibrous and stringy.

In order to preserve the quality of mushrooms, it's essential to:

- Proper storage is key to extending the shelf life and maintaining the quality of mushrooms, as previously discussed. As a result, you should choose the approach that best fits your requirements and tastes and adhere to each method's instructions. For instance, if you need to preserve fresh mushrooms, you should use them within a week and store them in the refrigerator in an open plastic or paper bag. Dried mushrooms should be used within a year or longer after being stored in sealed containers in a cold, dark environment.

- Use them carefully: Before using your mushrooms, make sure they are of a high grade and throw away any that are tainted or rotten. Additionally, you should only wash or rinse them just before cooking, since cleaning them by hand might cause the taste to fade and the water to absorb. Additionally, be sure to fully cook them since heat may remove certain potentially hazardous compounds found in some mushrooms. Additionally, as raw mushrooms might be poisonous or indigestible, you should avoid eating them.

- Ultimately, although mushrooms provide a variety of health advantages and gastronomic pleasures, you should consume them sensibly and securely. But you should also be aware of the possible dangers and adverse consequences associated with eating mushrooms, particularly wild ones. It's important to properly identify mushrooms and to never consume those that are unknown or harmful. In addition, if you are pregnant or nursing, have any allergies, or have any medical issues, you should speak with your doctor before consuming mushrooms. Additionally, you should keep an eye on how much you consume and how you respond to mushrooms. If you encounter any unfavorable symptoms, you should see a doctor.

Wonderful edible mushrooms may be picked, conserved, and kept in a variety of ways. You may prolong the shelf life of your mushrooms and preserve their quality by adhering to these pointers and recommendations.

Part 2: The Best Edible Mushrooms to Forage

Chapter 4: The Culinary Mushrooms: Delicious and Nutritious

In addition to being enthralling and adaptable, mushrooms are also tasty and nourishing items that may improve any recipe. It might be challenging to decide which mushrooms to use and how to prepare them, however, since there are so many different kinds available. This chapter will provide an introduction to a few of the most well-known and accessible edible mushrooms, along with details on their taste and texture qualities and preparation advice.

Porcini mushroom

The most popular and widely available edible mushrooms

- **Button mushrooms**, also referred to as white mushrooms, are the most accessible and affordable varieties available. Their texture is firm and crisp, and their taste is moderate and earthy. They work well in stir-fries, salads, soups, and sauces, among other dishes.

Button mushrooms

- **Brown mushrooms**, also referred to as baby bellas or creminis, are a kind of button mushroom with a richer taste and a darker hue. Their texture is luscious and soft, and their taste is meaty and nutty. They work well for stuffing, sautéing, roasting, and grilling.

Brown mushrooms

- **Portobello mushrooms**: Also referred to as portabella mushrooms, they are huge, mature cremini mushrooms with a taste closer to meat. Their taste is earthy and smokey, and their texture is chewy, like steak. They are perfect for marinating, broiling, baking, and grilling.

Portobello mushroom

- Native to East Asia, **shiitake mushrooms** have a deep, umami-rich, smokey taste. They feature a dark, scaly crown and a meaty, luscious feel. Asian dishes, including soups, stir-fries, noodles, and dumplings, often include them.

Shiitake mushroom

-

- **Oyster mushrooms**: They have a small stem or none at all, with a cap that resembles an oyster. They are colored white, gray, brown, or pink, among other hues. Their texture is silky, and their taste is somewhat nutty.

Oysters Mushroom

They may be fried, baked, grilled, or roasted, making them a flexible culinary tool.

- **Enoki mushrooms** are white, slender mushrooms with tiny caps and long stems. They have a crisp, crispy texture and a moderate, somewhat sweet taste. Asian cuisine often uses them, especially in salads and soups.

Enoki mushrooms

- **Chanterelle mushrooms**: These are trumpet-shaped mushrooms that are yellow, orange, or white in color, and their caps may be smooth or wavy. They have a soft, moist texture with a taste that is fruity and spicy. Gourmet cooking often uses them, particularly in French and Italian recipes.

Chanterelle mushroom

- **Morel mushrooms** are cone-shaped, brown, yellow, or black mushrooms with a texture akin to honeycomb. They are porous and spongy, with a taste that is earthy and nutty. Lovers of mushrooms, they are highly valued and often found in fine dining meals.

Morel mushroom

-
- **Porcini mushrooms** are a kind of mushroom that has a stem and a cap, but behind the top are tubes or pores that serve as gills. They are chewy and meaty, with a pronounced nutty taste. Italian food often uses them, especially in pastas and risottos.

Porcini mushrooms 2

- **Truffle mushrooms**: These are the subterranean fruiting bodies of certain fungus, not really mushrooms. They have a hard, waxy texture and a strong, musky, fragrant taste. They are quite costly and regarded as a delicacy. For taste and fragrance, they are often shaved or grated over food.

The flavor and texture profiles of each mushroom

Here are some further facts on the taste and texture qualities of each mushroom, along with some examples of recipes that go well with them, to help you pick and utilize the proper mushrooms for your meals:

- Button mushrooms: These may enhance or balance other tastes in a meal with their mild, earthy flavor. They may provide some bite and contrast to smooth or creamy meals because of their robust, crisp texture. Button mushrooms are a great complement to a number of recipes, including pizza, burgers, quiches, soups, risottos, omelets, and gravies.
- Cremini mushrooms: These may give a meal some depth and richness because of their meaty, nutty taste. Their juicy, soft nature makes them excellent at soaking up marinades and sauces. Cremini mushrooms go great with a

variety of foods, including mushroom stroganoff, lasagna, spaghetti, stuffed peppers, mushroom pot pie, and salad.

Cremini mushrooms

- Portobello mushrooms: These may give a meal a filling, robust flavor thanks to their earthy, smoky flavor. They may be eaten as a main meal or as a meat replacement because of their chewy, steak-like texture. Portobello mushroom burgers, fajitas, sandwiches, caprese, roasts, and soups are a few recipes that suit the vegetarian protein source nicely.

- Shiitake mushrooms: These may provide a meal with a savory and nuanced flavor thanks to their rich, smoky, and umami flavor. When cooked, their meaty, luscious texture allows them to retain their moisture and form. Foods like shiitake mushroom soup, stir-fried, noodle meals, dumplings, tempura, and sushi are some that go well with shiitake mushrooms.

- The mild, nutty taste of oyster mushrooms makes them a great element to combine with other ingredients in a meal. When fried or roasted, its delicate, velvety texture may become crispy and crunchy. Oyster mushroom soup, oyster curry, oyster tacos, oyster mushroom risotto, oyster mushroom chips, and oyster mushroom salad are a few recipes that go well with oyster mushrooms.

- Enoki mushrooms: They may give a meal a touch of freshness and lightness with their gentle, somewhat sweet taste. Their crisp and crunchy texture may provide a little texture and contrast to salads and soups. Oyster mushroom soup, salad, wrap, sandwich, omelet, and sushi are a few recipes that go well with enoki mushrooms.

- The fruity, spicy taste of chanterelle mushrooms may add some brightness and spiciness to a meal. When cooked, their soft, juicy texture may leak some juice. Chanterelle mushroom soup, spaghetti, risotto, pizza, quiche, and sauce are a few recipes that go well with chanterelle mushrooms.

- Morel mushrooms: These may provide additional depth and warmth to a meal with their nutty, earthy taste. Their texture is porous and spongy, making them excellent in absorbing liquids and tastes. Morel mushroom soup, morel mushroom sauce, morel mushroom omelets, morel mushroom chicken, morel mushroom asparagus, and morel mushroom bread pudding are some foods that go well with morel mushrooms.

- Porcini mushrooms: These provide a powerful, nutty taste to food that may make it more intense and rich. When cooked, their chewy, meaty texture helps them maintain their firmness and form. Porcini mushroom soup, porcini mushroom ravioli, porcini mushroom risotto, porcini mushroom polenta, and porcini mushroom steak are a few recipes that go well with porcini mushrooms.

- The strong, musky, fragrant taste of truffle mushrooms may give a meal a touch of refinement and richness. Their tough, waxy texture allows them to be grated or shaved to add taste and scent to food. The following are some recipes that go well with truffle mushrooms: truffle mushroom pizza, risotto, pasta, eggs, cheese, and popcorn.

Wonderful meals that can be enjoyed in a variety of ways include mushrooms.

The culinary uses and recipes for each mushroom

- The most affordable and widely available mushrooms on the market are button mushrooms. Their texture is firm and crisp, and their taste is moderate and earthy. They work well in stir-fries, salads, soups, and sauces, among other dishes. There are several dishes that call for button mushrooms, including burgers, quiches, omelets, pizzas, risottos, soups, and gravies.

- Button mushrooms with a richer taste and a darker hue are known as cremini mushrooms. Their texture is luscious and soft, and their taste is meaty and nutty. They work well for stuffing, sautéing, roasting, and grilling. Cremini mushrooms may be found in a variety of dishes, including mushroom stroganoff, lasagna, spaghetti, stuffed peppers, pot pie, and salad.

- Portobello mushrooms: These are huge, mature cremini mushrooms with a taste closer to flesh. Their taste is earthy and smokey, and their texture is chewy, like steak. They are perfect for marinating, broiling, baking, and grilling. Portobello mushrooms may be found in a variety of dishes, including roast, burgers, fajitas, sandwiches, caprese, roast potatoes, and soup.

- Native to East Asia, shiitake mushrooms have a deep, umami-rich, smokey taste. They feature a dark, scaly crown and a meaty, luscious feel. Asian dishes, including soups, stir-fries, noodles, and dumplings, often include them. The following are some dishes that make use of shiitake mushrooms: sushi, tempura, dumplings, noodles, soup, stir-fry, and noodles with shiitake mushrooms.

- Oyster mushrooms: They have a small stem or none at all, with a cap that resembles an oyster. They are colored white, gray, brown, or pink, among other hues. Their texture is silky, and their taste is somewhat nutty. They may be fried, baked, grilled, or roasted, making them a flexible culinary tool. Recipes such as oyster mushroom soup, oyster mushroom curry, oyster mushroom tacos, oyster mushroom risotto, oyster mushroom chips, and oyster mushroom salad all call for oyster mushrooms.

- Enoki mushrooms are white, slender mushrooms with tiny caps and long stems. They have a crisp, crispy texture and a moderate, somewhat sweet taste. Asian cuisine often uses them, especially in salads and soups. Omelets, sushi, wraps, sandwiches, soups, salads, and omelets made with enoki mushrooms are just a few of the dishes that call for them.

- Chanterelle mushrooms: These are trumpet-shaped mushrooms that are yellow, orange, or white in color, and their caps may be smooth or wavy. They have a soft, moist texture with a taste that is fruity and spicy. Gourmet cooking often uses them, particularly in French and Italian recipes. Chanterelle mushrooms may be used in a variety of dishes, including quiche, pizza, risotto, soup, pasta, and sauce.

- Morel mushrooms are cone-shaped, brown, yellow, or black mushrooms with a texture akin to honeycomb. They are porous and spongy, with a taste that is earthy and nutty. I love mushrooms, they are highly valued and often found in fine dining meals. Morel mushrooms may be used in a variety of dishes, including morel soup, morel sauce, morel chicken, morel asparagus, morel bread pudding, and morel omelets.

- Porcini mushrooms are a kind of mushroom that has a stem and a cap, but behind the top are tubes or pores that serve as gills. They are chewy and meaty, with a pronounced nutty taste. Italian food often uses them, especially in pastas and risottos. Porcini mushrooms may be found in a variety of dishes, including porcini mushroom ravioli, porcini mushroom soup, porcini mushroom spaghetti, porcini mushroom risotto, and porcini mushroom steak.

- Truffle mushrooms: These are the subterranean fruiting bodies of certain fungus, not really mushrooms. They have a hard, waxy texture and a strong, musky, fragrant taste. They are quite costly and regarded as a delicacy. For taste and fragrance, they are often shaved or grated over food. Truffle mushrooms may be used in a variety of dishes, including truffle mushroom cheese, truffle mushroom popcorn, pizza, risotto, pasta, and eggs.

The nutritional and culinary values of each mushroom

- Button mushrooms are rich in protein, fiber, and several vitamins and minerals, including phosphorus, potassium, iron, niacin, and pantothenic acid, but low in calories, fat, and salt. They may support immunity, reduce cholesterol, minimize oxidative stress, and help control blood pressure. Additionally, they have a subtle, earthy taste that works well with other components in a meal.

- In terms of nutrition, cremini mushrooms are comparable to button mushrooms; however, they have a slightly greater concentration of selenium, riboflavin, and vitamin B. They may promote healthy nerves, metabolism, and thyroid function. They may also give a meal some depth and richness because of their meaty, nutty taste.

- Portobello mushrooms: These are nutritionally comparable to button mushrooms but have a little bit of vitamin D, which is uncommon in plant diets. They may support immunological responses, calcium absorption, and bone health. Additionally, they have an earthy, smokey flavor that may give a meal a filling, robust flavor.

- Shiitake mushrooms have a low calorie, fat, and salt content but a high protein, fiber content and a variety of vitamins and minerals, including zinc, copper, selenium, manganese, and vitamin B. They may improve immunity, liver function, and skin health, in addition to lowering blood pressure, cholesterol, and inflammation. Additionally, they contain a deep, smokey, umami flavor that gives food a delicious, nuanced flavor.

- Oyster mushrooms are rich in protein, fiber, and several vitamins and minerals, including iron, zinc, and vitamin B. They are also low in calories, fat, and salt. They may aid in lowering cholesterol, preventing anemia, and enhancing blood circulation. Additionally, they have a subtle, nutty taste that goes well with other components of a meal.

- Enoki mushrooms are rich in protein, fiber, and many vitamins and minerals, including folate, vitamin B, vitamin B, and vitamin B. They are low in calories, fat, and salt. They can promote nerve health, stop neural tube defects, and control blood pressure. Additionally, they have a mild, somewhat sweet taste that may give food a little freshness and lightness.

- Chanterelle mushrooms are rich in protein, fiber, and several vitamins and minerals, including potassium, copper, iron, vitamin C, vitamin D, and vitamin K. They are also low in calories, fat, and salt. They may improve blood coagulation, bone health, immunity, and iron absorption. They may add some brightness and spice to a meal with their sweet and peppery taste.

- Morel mushrooms: These may provide additional depth and warmth to a meal with their nutty, earthy taste. Their texture is porous and spongy, making them excellent at absorbing liquids and tastes. Morel mushrooms may be used in a variety of dishes, including morel soup, morel sauce, morel chicken, morel asparagus, morel bread pudding, and morel omelets.

- Porcini mushrooms: These provide a powerful, nutty taste to food that may make it more intense and rich. When cooked, their chewy, meaty texture helps them maintain their firmness and form. Porcini mushrooms may be found in a variety of dishes, including porcini mushroom ravioli, porcini mushroom soup, porcini mushroom spaghetti, porcini mushroom risotto, and porcini mushroom steak.

- The strong, musky, fragrant taste of truffle mushrooms may give a meal a touch of refinement and richness. Their tough, waxy texture allows them to be grated or shaved to add taste and scent to food. Truffle mushrooms may be used in a variety of dishes, including truffle mushroom cheese, truffle mushroom popcorn, pizza, risotto, pasta, and eggs.

The nutritional and culinary values of each mushroom

Each mushroom has various nutritional and culinary qualities, including:

- Morel mushrooms are rich in protein, fiber, and many vitamins and minerals, including iron, copper, manganese, zinc, vitamin B, and vitamin B12. They are also low in calories, fat, and salt. They may improve immunity, liver function, and skin health, in addition to lowering blood pressure, cholesterol, and inflammation. Additionally, they have an earthy, nutty taste that may add complexity and warmth to a meal.

- Porcini mushrooms are rich in protein, fiber, and several vitamins and minerals, including copper, selenium, manganese, potassium, phosphorus, and vitamin B. They are also low in calories, fat, and salt. They may promote healthy nerves, metabolism, and thyroid function. Additionally, they have a robust, nutty taste that may enhance the richness and depth of a meal.

- Truffle mushrooms are rich in protein, fiber, and many vitamins and minerals, including iron, calcium, magnesium, zinc, vitamin C, and vitamin K. They are also low in calories, fat, and salt. They may support enhanced immune system performance, bone health, and blood circulation. They may also give a meal a touch of opulence and refinement with their strong, musky, fragrant taste.

The best practices and tips for cooking and serving mushrooms

The following are some of the top methods and suggestions for preparing and presenting mushrooms:

- Select firm, fresh mushrooms. Avoid slimy, shriveled, or moldy mushrooms when purchasing or gathering them. Instead, aim for firm, dry, and fresh mushrooms. Steer clear of mushrooms with black stains, splits, or bruising. Select mushrooms that are neither speckled nor discolored, but rather have a consistent, natural hue. Select mushrooms with an earthy, fresh scent rather than one that is musty or unpleasant.

- Because they are very perishable and prone to deterioration, mushrooms should be stored carefully. To preserve their quality and safety, they should be kept appropriately. Use the mushrooms within a week after storing them in an open plastic bag or paper bag in the refrigerator. Before storing mushrooms, don't wash or slice them since this will cause them to absorb water and lose taste. Mushrooms should not be kept in plastic wrap or sealed containers since this might retain moisture and lead to rotting.

- Mushrooms are sensitive and rapidly absorb water, so handle them with care. As a result, before cooking, they should be quickly and carefully cleaned. Using a moist cloth, paper towel, or soft brush to wipe off mushrooms is the best method for cleaning them. As an alternative, you may give them a brief rinse under cold running water; just don't soak or scrub them too hard. Use a paper towel or rag to pat them dry after washing.

- Slice or chop mushrooms evenly: Because they vary in size and form, mushrooms may need to be sliced or chopped before cooking. Cut the mushrooms into consistent pieces, following the instructions or your own preferences, to ensure equal frying and browning. Depending on the size and variety, you may alternatively leave the mushrooms whole or cut them in half. If the stem is thick or woody, however, you should always cut it or remove it if you are creating stuffed mushrooms.

- Cook the mushrooms fully since uncooked mushrooms may lose taste and become brown or squishy due to the enzymes and other compounds they contain. As a result, they must be boiled sufficiently to eliminate these compounds and enzymes, as well as any dangerous microorganisms or poisons. Mushrooms get more taste, texture, and nutrition when they are cooked. Depending on the kind and number of mushrooms, the cooking process and duration may vary, but in general, it takes a few minutes to several hours.

- Because mushrooms contain a lot of water, they may leak a lot of liquid when cooked, so use high heat and plenty of oil. For this reason, they need to be cooked over high heat with enough fat to encourage searing and caramelizing rather than steaming and boiling. Rich and deep flavor and a crispy, golden crust may also be developed in mushrooms by using high heat and oil. Using butter or oil—or both—or a mix of the two will depend on the recipe and your preferences. But, you don't want to pack the pan too full since this will allow the temperature to drop and the mushrooms to stew in their own juices.

- Make sure to properly season the mushrooms since they have a subtle, earthy taste that works nicely with other ingredients in a meal. For the finest flavor and fragrance, they should thus be well-seasoned. Salt, pepper, onion, garlic, mustard, dill, oregano, nutmeg, basil, paprika, parsley, sage, rosemary, or thyme may all be used to season mushrooms. Lemon juice, vinegar, or wine are examples of acids that you may use to brighten and balance the richness of the dish. To add some creaminess and crunch, you may also add some cheese, cream, or nuts.

- Serve mushrooms hot or cold: Depending on the cuisine and your own preferences, mushrooms may be served either way. Serve hot mushrooms as a filler, topping, side dish, or main entrée. You may eat cold mushrooms as a snack, salad, wrap, or sandwich. Mushrooms may also be reheated, however, doing so may change their taste and texture. Depending on the kind and quantity of mushrooms, you may reheat them in a pan, toaster oven, oven, or microwave.

Chapter 5: The Medicinal Mushrooms: Healing and Healthy

This chapter will provide an overview of some of the most potent and advantageous medicinal mushrooms, outlining their qualities and health advantages.

The most potent and beneficial medicinal mushrooms

Among the strongest and most advantageous medicinal mushrooms are:

- Reishi:

Reishi Mushroom

-

Also referred to as Ganoderma lucidum, this fungus is revered in traditional Chinese medicine as the "king of mushrooms" or the "mushroom of immortality." It tastes unpleasant and has a kidney-shaped, bright crimson cap. Its immune-stimulating, anti-inflammatory, anti-tumor, antiviral, and anti-diabetic properties make it popular. In addition, it may help reduce stress, blood pressure, and cholesterol while enhancing mood and quality of sleep.

- Chaga: Also called Inonotus obliquus, this mushroom is a parasitic fungus that grows on birch trees instead of being a true mushroom. It looks like burned charcoal—it's hard, cracked, and black. Antioxidants, polysaccharides, and betulinic acid, which are abundant in it, may aid in the battle against cancer, inflammation, and oxidative stress.

Chaga Mushroom

- In addition, it may guard the kidneys and liver and help control blood sugar, cholesterol, and the immunological system.

- Cordyceps: Also called Cordyceps sinensis, this mushroom is really a parasitic fungus that combines the characteristics of a caterpillar. It is shaped like a worm—long, thin, and segmented. It is well known for its aphrodisiac, energy-boosting, and stamina-boosting properties.

Cordyceps Mushroom

- In addition, it may help prevent diabetes and renal disease and enhance heart health, blood circulation, oxygen absorption, lung function, and heart health.

- Hericium erinaceus, also known as the "lion's mane," is a unique-looking mushroom that resembles a white pom-pom. Its fruiting body is covered in long, shaggy spines that cascade downward. It is well known for its ability to strengthen the brain, regenerate nerves, and improve memory.

Lion's mane mushroom

- It may also help prevent neurological disorders like Parkinson's and Alzheimer's, as well as enhance mood, mental health, and cognitive function.

- **Turkey Tail**:

Turkey Tail Mushroom

- Also called Trametes versicolor, this mushroom grows on dead or rotting wood and has a fan- or bracket-shaped cap. It looks striped and multicolored, like the tail of a turkey. With its ability to modulate immunity and fight cancer, it is one of the most studied and popular medicinal mushrooms. In addition, it may help reduce inflammation and infections while promoting better digestion, gut health, and the microbiota.

- **Shiitake**: Often referred to as Lentinula edodes, this fungus is among the most well-liked and often eaten edible mushrooms worldwide. Its cap is umbrella-shaped and brown, and its texture is meaty and luscious. With anti-viral, anti-bacterial, anti-fungal, and anti-tumor properties, it is also a powerful medicinal mushroom. In addition, it may strengthen immunity and enhance liver function while lowering blood pressure, blood sugar, and cholesterol.

- **Maitake**: sometimes called Grifola frondosa, this fungus is sometimes referred to in Japanese as "hen of the woods" or "dancing mushroom." Its form is big, cluster-like, and frond-like, like the feathers of a hen or the skirt of a dancer. In addition to being a tasty and nourishing edible mushroom, it has potent therapeutic properties that include anti-obesity, anti-diabetic, and anti-cancer properties. In addition, it may help avoid metabolic syndrome and cardiovascular disease and regulate blood sugar, hormones, and the immune system.

Maitake Musroom

The health benefits and properties of each mushroom

Here is some further data about each mushroom, along with some useful advice and safety measures, to help you comprehend and value their many health advantages and qualities:

- Reishi: This fungus is rich in bioactive substances that may influence the immune system, stop the development and spread of cancer cells, lessen pain and inflammation, and protect the kidneys and liver. These substances include polysaccharides, triterpenes, sterols, and peptides. Reishi has been shown to enhance the functioning of the neurological, respiratory, and cardiovascular systems, as well as reduce blood pressure, cholesterol, and blood sugar. Reishi has been shown to help balance hormones, boost mood and mental health, and increase sleep quality. Typically, reishi is consumed as a tea, extract, powder, or pill. The suggested daily dose varies according to the type and concentration, from grams to grams. Although reishi is typically safe and well-tolerated, some individuals may have blood thinning effects, allergic reactions, unsettled stomachs, or dry mouths, throats, or noses. Additionally, reishi may interact with immunosuppressants, anticoagulants, or hypoglycemic medicines. Consequently, before using reishi, it is best to speak with a doctor, particularly if you have a medical problem or are on any medications.

- Chaga: This fungus has one of the highest concentrations of antioxidants, particularly melanin, which may shield DNA from oxidative damage, scavenge free radicals, and prevent damage from free radicals. Polysaccharides, betulinic acid, and other phytochemicals found in chaga have the ability to boost the immune system, cause cancer cells to undergo apoptosis, reduce inflammation and infection, and alter cholesterol and blood sugar levels. In addition to enhancing the health and look of the skin and hair, chaga may help shield the liver and kidneys from toxins and harm. Typically, chaga is consumed as a tea, extract, powder, or pill. The suggested daily dose varies according to the type and concentration, from grams to grams. Though most individuals find chaga to be safe and well-tolerated, others may have allergic reactions, unsettled stomachs, or hypoglycemic consequences. Additionally, there is a chance that chaga will interfere with some drugs, such as immunosuppressants, anticoagulants, or hypoglycemic medicines. Consequently, before using chaga, it is best to speak with a doctor, particularly if you have a medical problem or are on any medications.

- Cordyceps: This mushroom may improve the body's synthesis and use of blood, oxygen, and energy. It also includes polysaccharides, cordycepin, and cordycepic acid. Additionally, cordyceps may boost libido and sexual performance while also enhancing the heart, lungs, brain, and muscles' endurance and function. In addition, cordyceps may help prevent or cure diabetes and renal disease, as well as strengthen the immune system and combat infections and inflammation. Typically, cordyceps is consumed as a tea, extract, powder, or pill. The suggested daily dose varies according to the type and concentration, from grams to grams. Though most individuals find cordyceps to be safe and well-tolerated, some people may have allergic reactions, unsettled stomachs, or bleeding problems. Additionally, cordyceps may interfere with some drugs, including immunosuppressants, anticoagulants, and hypoglycemic medicines. Consequently, before consuming cordyceps, it is best to speak with a doctor, particularly if you have a medical condition or are on any medications.

- Lion's Mane: This mushroom has two kinds of chemicals called hericenones and erinacines, which may promote the production and release of nerve growth factor (NGF), a protein necessary for neuron survival, development, and maintenance. In addition, lion's mane has been shown to improve brain plasticity and function, as well as to prevent or cure neurodegenerative illnesses including Parkinson's and Alzheimer's. In addition to enhancing mood and mental health, lion's mane helps lessen the signs of anxiety and despair. Typically, lion's mane is consumed as a tea, extract, powder, or pill. The suggested daily dose varies according to the type and concentration, from grams to grams. Although lion's mane is typically safe and well-tolerated, some individuals may irritate their skin, have allergic reactions, or have digestive problems. Additionally, several drugs, including anticoagulants, antidepressants, and anticonvulsants, may interact with Lion's Mane. Consequently, before using Lion's Mane, it is best to speak with a doctor, particularly if you have a medical problem or are on any medications.

- Turkey Tail: This fungus has two kinds of polysaccharides called polysaccharide-K (PSK) and polysaccharopeptide (PSP), which have the ability to influence the immune system, stimulate macrophages and natural killer cells, and stop the spread and proliferation of cancer cells. Turkey tail, which contains prebiotics—substances that nourish the good bacteria in the intestines—can also aid in enhancing gut health, digestion, and the microbiota. Additionally, turkey tail may be used to prevent or cure gastrointestinal system infections and inflammation, including colitis, ulcers, and irritable bowel syndrome. Typically, turkey tail is consumed as a tea, extract, powder, or pill. The suggested daily dose varies according to the type and concentration, from grams to grams. Though most individuals find turkey tail to be safe and well-tolerated, others may develop adverse responses, unsettled stomachs, or effects that thin the blood. Additionally, Turkey Tail may interfere with immunosuppressive drugs, anticoagulants, or hypoglycemic medicines. Consequently, before using Turkey Tail, it is best to speak with a doctor, particularly if you have a medical condition or are on any medications.

The medicinal uses and preparations for each mushroom

Each mushroom has a variety of therapeutic applications and preparations, such as:

- Reishi: This fungus is used to treat a number of illnesses, including cancer, hepatitis, liver cirrhosis, allergies, asthma, bronchitis, hypertension, hypercholesterolemia, and diabetes. Reishi is also used to promote lifespan, lower stress, and strengthen immunity. You may make reishi as a powder, pill, tincture, decoction, tea, or extract. To prepare reishi tea, place dried or fresh reishi slices in water, let it simmer for about an hour, filter it, and then consume the beverage. Reishi slices may be boiled in water for about two hours to make reishi decoction, which is then reduced to a concentrated liquid. To make reishi tincture, soak reishi slices in alcohol for about two weeks, strain the liquid, and store it in a dark container. Reishi extract may be prepared by using alcohol, boiling water, or other solvents to extract the active ingredients from the reishi, then drying and powdering the leftover material. One way to make reishi powder is to finely grind dried reishi slices and then mix or encapsulate them with water or other liquids. Reishi capsules are prepared by packing reishi powder or extract into vegetarian or gelatin capsules and closing the container.

- Chaga: This fungus is used to treat a number of illnesses, including cancer, diabetes, renal disease, ulcers, gastritis, colitis, inflammation, and infections. In addition, chaga is utilized to preserve the kidneys and liver, boost immunity, and improve skin and hair. You may make chaga as a powder, pill, tincture, decoction, tea, or extract. Making chaga tea involves steeping fresh or dried chaga powder or chunks in hot water for a few minutes, filtering the resulting liquid, and then drinking it. Boiling chaga chunks or powder in water for around an hour and then condensing the liquid to a concentrated state is how chaga decoction is created. Making chaga tincture involves soaking chaga powder or chunks in alcohol for about one month, straining the mixture, and keeping it in a dark container. Using hot water, alcohol, or other solvents to extract the active chemicals from chaga, followed by drying and crushing the residue into a powder, is how chaga extract is created. Dried chaga chunks or powder may be ground into a fine powder and then mixed or enclosed in water or other liquids to make chaga powder. Gelatin or vegetarian capsules may be filled with chaga powder or extract, sealed, and used as chaga capsules.

- Cordyceps: This fungus is used to treat a number of illnesses, including cancer, respiratory disorders, renal disease, anemia, weariness, weakness, and impotence. Additionally, cordyceps is utilized to increase libido, sexual performance, vitality, and stamina. You may make a tea, decoction, tincture, extract, powder, or capsule out of cordyceps. To make cordyceps tea, steep either fresh or dried cordyceps in hot water for a few minutes, filter, and enjoy the resulting beverage. To make a decoction of cordyceps, boil the leaves in water for a few minutes, then reduce the liquid until it becomes concentrated. To make a tincture, soak cordyceps in alcohol for about two weeks, strain the liquid, and store it in a dark container. Using hot water, alcohol, or other solvents to extract the active chemicals from the cordyceps, followed by drying and grinding the residue into a powder, is how cordyceps extract is manufactured. Dried cordyceps may be ground into a fine powder and then mixed or enclosed in water or other liquids to make cordyceps powder. Cordyceps extract or powder may be added to gelatin or vegetarian capsules, which can then be sealed and used as a cordyceps capsule.

- Lion's Mane: This fungus is used to treat a number of illnesses, including nerve damage, depression, anxiety, dementia, Alzheimer's disease, and Parkinson's disease. Additionally, lion's mane is utilized to improve mental wellness, nerve development, and brain function. You may make a tea, decoction, tincture, extract, powder, or capsule out of lion's mane. To make Lion's Mane tea, steep either fresh or dried lion's mane in boiling water for a few minutes, filter, and enjoy the resulting beverage. To make a decoction of lion's mane, boil the mane for about one hour, then reduce the liquid to a concentrated form. To make lion's mane tincture, soak the mane in alcohol for about two weeks, strain the liquid, and store it in a dark container. Using hot water, alcohol, or other solvents to extract the active chemicals from lion's mane, followed by drying and grinding the residue into a powder, is how lion's mane extract is created. Dried lion's mane may be ground into a fine powder and then mixed with or enclosed in water or other liquids to create lion's mane powder. Making lion's mane capsules involves adding lion's mane powder or extract to vegetarian or gelatin capsules, capping the container, and then pressing the lid shut.

- Turkey Tail: This mushroom is used to treat a number of illnesses, including cancer, hepatitis, liver cirrhosis, ulcers, inflammation, gastritis, and colitis. Moreover, turkey tail is utilized to strengthen immunity, promote gastrointestinal health, and either prevent or cure HPV infection in humans. You may make tea, decoctions, tinctures, extracts, powders, or capsules from turkey tail. Fresh or dried turkey tail may be steeped in boiling water for a few minutes to make turkey tail tea. The liquid can then be strained and consumed. Boiling turkey tail in water for around one hour and then condensing the liquid to a concentrated state is how turkey tail decoction is created. To make Turkey Tail Tincture, soak turkey tail in alcohol for about two weeks, strain the liquid, and store it in a dark container. Using hot water, alcohol, or other solvents to extract the active ingredients from turkey tail, followed by drying and grinding the residue into a powder, is how turkey tail extract is created. Dried turkey tail may be ground into a fine powder and then mixed or enclosed in water or other drinks to create turkey tail powder. Turkey tail powder or extract may be added to vegetarian or gelatin capsules, which can then be sealed. This process creates a turkey tail capsule.

- Shiitake: This mushroom is used to treat a number of illnesses, including cancer, hepatitis, liver cirrhosis, hyperlipidemia, hypertension, infections, and inflammation. In addition, shiitake is utilized to control cholesterol, strengthen immunity, and safeguard the kidneys and liver. You may make shiitake as a powder, pill, tincture, tea, decoction, or extract. To prepare shiitake tea, soak dried or fresh shiitake in boiling water for a few minutes, drain, and then enjoy the infusion. Boiling shiitake in water for around an hour and then condensing the liquid to a concentrated form is how shiitake decoction is created. To make shiitake tincture, soak shiitake in alcohol for about two weeks, strain, and store the liquid in a dark container. Using hot water, alcohol, or other solvents to extract the active components from shiitake, followed by drying and grinding the residue into a powder, is how shiitake extract is manufactured. Dried shiitake mushrooms may be ground into a fine powder and then encapsulated or combined with liquids to make shiitake powder. To make shiitake capsules, add shiitake powder or extract to vegetarian or gelatin capsules, seal, and proceed.

- Maitake: This mushroom is used to treat a number of illnesses, including cancer, diabetes, hyperlipidemia, hypertension, and obesity. In addition, maitake helps control blood sugar, boost immunity, and either prevent or cure metabolic syndrome and cardiovascular disease. You may make maitake as a powder, pill, tincture, decoction, tea, or extract. Fresh or dried maitake may be steeped in boiling water for a few minutes to make maitake tea. The liquid can then be strained and consumed. To make maitake decoction, boil the mushrooms in water for about one hour, then reduce the liquid until it becomes a concentrated syrup. To make maitake tincture, soak the mushrooms in alcohol for about two weeks, strain the liquid, and store it in a dark container. Using hot water, alcohol, or other solvents to extract the active components from maitake, followed by drying and grinding the residue into a powder, is how maitake extract is created. Dried maitake may be ground into a fine powder and then mixed or enclosed in water or other liquids to make maitake powder. A maitake capsule is created by packing powdered or extracted maitake inside vegetarian or gelatin capsules and closing the container.

The scientific evidence and research behind the health benefits and properties of each mushroom

Here are some references and sources that back up the claims and conclusions about each mushroom, along with certain restrictions and difficulties with the study, to help you comprehend and appreciate the scientific evidence and investigation behind the health advantages and characteristics of each mushroom:

- Reishi: Several studies and reviews have shown how reishi and its bioactive substances, including polysaccharides, triterpenes, and peptides, have immunomodulatory, anti-inflammatory, anti-tumor, anti-viral, and anti-diabetic properties. For example, reishi was shown to dramatically lower blood glucose levels in people with type 2 diabetes in a meta-analysis of randomized controlled trials including participants. A different meta-analysis of participant-initiated randomized controlled studies revealed that reishi greatly enhanced cancer patients' immune systems and quality of life. The lack of standardization, quality control, and safety assessment of reishi products, the heterogeneity and inconsistent study designs and outcomes, and the requirement for more extensive and rigorous clinical trials to validate the effectiveness and mechanism of action of reishi are some of the research's limitations and challenges.

- Chaga: Numerous research studies and reviews have shown the anti-inflammatory, anti-tumor, anti-oxidant, and anti-diabetic properties of chaga, as well as the bioactive chemicals it contains, including polysaccharides, betulinic acid, and melanin. For instance, chaga extract dramatically reduced the disease's biochemical markers and clinical symptoms in a research involving psoriasis patients. In a different trial, chaga extract dramatically improved liver and kidney function and lowered blood glucose, cholesterol, and triglyceride levels in individuals with diabetes mellitus. The lack of standardization, quality control, and safety assessment of chaga products; the potential toxicity and negative effects of chaga; and the necessity for additional mechanistic and pharmacological studies to clarify the mode of action of chaga are some of the research's limitations and challenges.

- Cordyceps: A multitude of research and reviews have shown the aphrodisiac, energy-enhancing, stamina-boosting, and anti-aging properties of cordyceps and their bioactive constituents, including polysaccharides, cordycepin, and cordycepic acid. For instance, cordyceps greatly enhanced the physical performance, oxygen consumption, and quality of life of a group of aged, healthy volunteers in a study. Cordyceps was shown to dramatically enhance sexual function, desire, and pleasure in another trial including individuals with sexual dysfunction. The origin, identity, and quality of cordyceps products are unpredictable and uncertain, the study methods and results are inconsistent and incomplete, and more thorough and robust clinical trials are required to confirm the safety and efficacy of cordyceps. These are just a few of the limitations and difficulties that the research faces.

- Lion's Mane: Several studies and reviews have shown how lion's mane and its bioactive constituents, such as erinacines and hericenones, have neuroprotective, neuroregenerative, and cognitively boosting properties. For instance, lion's mane dramatically enhanced the cognitive function and memory of patients in a trial involving moderate cognitive impairment. In a different study, individuals with peripheral nerve damage discovered that lion's mane greatly sped up their healing and regeneration of damaged nerves. The lack of standardization, quality control, and safety assessment of lion's mane products, the difficulty and complexity of isolating and identifying the active compounds of lion's mane, and the need for additional mechanistic and pharmacological studies to comprehend the mode of action of lion's mane are some of the research's limitations and challenges.

- Turkey Tail: A large body of research, including reviews, has shown the immunomodulatory, anti-viral, anti-cancer, and antibacterial properties of turkey tail and its bioactive constituents, including polysaccharide-K (PSK) and polysaccharopeptide (PSP). For instance, a meta-analysis of randomized controlled trials with participants revealed that PSK considerably raised the immune response and survival rate of cancer patients. In a different trial, individuals with HPV-positive cervical lesions had much smaller and fewer lesions overall, and the HPV infection cleared up more quickly when PSP was used. The variability and inconsistent quality and dosage of turkey tail products, the heterogeneity and bias of study designs and outcomes, and the requirement for more extensive and rigorous clinical trials to validate the efficacy and safety of turkey tail are some of the research's limitations and challenges.

- Shiitake: A number of investigations and reviews have shown that shiitake and its bioactive constituents, including lentinan, eritadenine, and lentinolic acid, have immunomodulatory, anti-tumor, anti-viral, anti-bacterial, and anti-fungal properties. For instance, shiitake dramatically enhanced immunological function, decreased inflammation, and lowered cholesterol in a study of healthy people. In another study, shiitake was shown to dramatically lower the viral load and improve liver function in individuals with chronic hepatitis B. The lack of standardization, quality control, and safety assessment of shiitake products, the possibility of shiitake toxicity and allergies, and the requirement for additional mechanistic and pharmacological research to clarify the mode of action of shiitake are some of the research's limitations and challenges.

- Maitake: Numerous research studies and reviews have shown the anti-obesity, anti-diabetic, and anti-cancer properties of maitake and its bioactive constituents, including D-fraction, SX-fraction, and beta-glucans. For instance, maitake D-fraction dramatically improved the immune response and decreased the adverse effects of chemotherapy in a trial involving patients with breast cancer. Another study with type 2 diabetic patients discovered that maitake SX-fraction greatly enhanced the patients' ability to manage their blood sugar and sensitivity to insulin. The small number and size of human clinical trials, the absence of standardization, quality control, and safety evaluation of maitake products, the possibility of hypoglycemia and blood thinning effects of maitake, and the requirement for additional mechanistic and pharmacological research to comprehend the mode of action of maitake are some of the research's limitations and challenges.

In addition to being delicious meals, mushrooms have therapeutic properties. Making educated decisions about utilizing them for your health and well-being is possible if you are aware of their medical applications, formulations, and supporting scientific data and research.

The precautions and contraindications for using medicinal mushrooms

The following are a few guidelines and avoidances while using medicinal mushrooms:

- Misidentification: When taking therapeutic mushrooms, misidentification is one of the most dangerous and possibly lethal dangers. While certain wild mushrooms may seem very similar to edible or therapeutic mushrooms, they are deadly or poisonous in the true sense. Seizures, coma, liver damage, renal failure, nausea, vomiting, diarrhea, abdominal discomfort, and even death may result from consuming these mushrooms. As a result, it's critical that you can identify the mushrooms you use properly and that you refrain from harvesting or consuming any that you are unsure about. Before using any mushroom, you should also get advice from a trustworthy expert, guide, or source. You should also carefully observe the dose directions.

- Contamination: Using therapeutic mushrooms carries an additional danger of contamination. Heavy metals, insecticides, pollutants, and poisons from the air, water, or soil where they grow may be absorbed or accumulated by mushrooms. These compounds have the potential to induce negative health consequences, including cancer, allergic responses, infections, and inflammation. Therefore, it is best to steer clear of mushrooms that have been exposed to or polluted by dangerous chemicals and instead choose mushrooms that are produced, farmed, or harvested organically from clean and safe places. Before utilizing mushrooms, make sure they are well cleaned, stored, and disposed of. Mushrooms that are moldy, spoiled, or damaged should be thrown out.

- negative effects: Using medicinal mushrooms has an additional risk of negative effects. Depending on the kind, quantity, and length of usage, mushrooms may affect your body in different ways. While some of these impacts could be advantageous, others might be unfavorable or dangerous. Anxiety reactions such as rash, itching, swelling, or trouble breathing; blood-thinning effects such as bleeding, bruises, or an increased risk of hemorrhage; hypoglycemic effects such as low blood sugar, dizziness, or fainting; or hormonal effects such as changes in menstrual cycle, fertility, or libido are some of the common side effects associated with using medicinal mushrooms. As a result, it's critical to keep an eye on how your body reacts to the medicinal mushrooms you take and modify the amount, frequency, or length of usage as necessary. Additionally, you must to cease taking medicinal mushrooms if you encounter any serious or enduring adverse effects, and get help from a doctor if required.

- Interactions: Using medicinal mushrooms has an additional risk of interactions. The absorption, metabolism, or effectiveness of other compounds—such as drugs, vitamins, herbs, or foods—can be impacted by interactions between mushrooms and other substances. While some of these interactions may be advantageous, others may be harmful or even deadly. The use of medicinal mushrooms frequently results in interactions with anticoagulants, such as increased bleeding risk or decreased clotting ability; immunosuppressants, such as decreased immune function or increased risk of infection; hypoglycemics, such as decreased blood sugar or increased sensitivity to insulin; and antidepressants, such as altered mood or mental state or increased risk of serotonin syndrome. Therefore, before taking medicinal mushrooms, make sure your doctor, pharmacist, or other healthcare professional is aware of any other medications you take and that there are no possible interactions. Additionally, you should refrain from combining medicinal mushrooms with drugs that might counteract or enhance their effects, or compromise their safcty.

Chapter 6: The Exotic Mushrooms: Rare and Remarkable

One of the planet's most interesting and varied species are mushrooms. They offer a diverse spectrum of nutritional advantages and ecological purposes, and they are available in an array of forms, sizes, colors, and textures. While some mushrooms are abundant and straightforward to locate, others are elusive and unusual. While some mushrooms are strange and exquisite, others are straightforward and unremarkable. We'll look at some of the strangest and most fascinating edible mushrooms found in North America in this chapter. These mushrooms will give your cooking repertoire a dash of adventure and exoticism in addition to being tasty and healthy.

Cremini mushrooms

The most unusual and intriguing edible mushrooms

Here are some of the most fascinating and peculiar edible mushrooms that can be found foraging in North America, along with information about their appearance and natural habitat:

- **Lion's Mane (Hericium erinaceus)**: This mushroom has long, hanging spines that resemble cream or white pom-poms. It grows in the temperate woods of North America, Europe, and Asia on hardwood trees, particularly beech, oak, and maple. Its texture is akin to that of crab or lobster, and its taste is mild, sweet, and meaty. It is also well-known for its therapeutic qualities, which include strengthening the immune system, memory, and nerve regeneration.

- **Bleeding Tooth (Hydnellum peckii)**:

-

- This mushroom has crimson drips coming out of its pores, giving it the appearance of a tooth or sponge. It grows on the ground in temperate and boreal forests in North America, Europe, and Asia, mainly under conifers. When it is young and fresh, it may be eaten, although it tastes harsh and peppery and might upset your stomach. Its ability to generate different hues of green, yellow, blue, and purple makes it more valuable for dyeing purposes.

- **Indigo Milk Cap (Lactarius indigo):**

Lactarius indigo Mushroom

- When sliced or wounded, this mushroom releases a blue milky or latex substance. Its cap, gills, and stem are all dark blue or indigo in color. It grows on the ground in the deciduous and mixed forests of eastern North America,

158

East Asia, and Central America, mainly under hardwoods. Its texture is hard and brittle, and its taste is moderate, nutty, and somewhat sweet. It may be consumed pickled, cooked, or raw.

- **Latticed Stinkhorn (Clathrus ruber)**: This mushroom starts out as a white, egg-shaped base and grows into a brilliant red, latticed, or basket-like structure.

Clathrus ruber

-
- It grows on the ground in warm temperate and subtropical parts of North America, Europe, Africa, Asia, and Australia, mainly on wood chips, mulch, or rich soil. Its greenish slime, which has an unpleasant odor, attracts flies and other insects, which aid in the spread of its

spores. When it's young and still within the egg, it may be eaten, but it tastes rubbery and bland and can make you sick or throw up.

- **Puffball (Basidiomycota)**: This category includes mushrooms without a cap, gills, or stem that are spherical, ball-like, or pear-like in form. They grow in a variety of habitats and places throughout North America, including on the ground, in wood, and in dung. When they are mature or disturbed, they expel the spores that are produced within their fruiting body in a plume of smoke.

Basidiomycota Mushroom

-
- When young and white inside, they are edible; when old and yellow or brown inside, they become toxic. Their texture is soft or spongy, and their taste is mild, mushroomy, or nutty.

- **Morel (Morchella spp.)**: This mushroom has a hollow, white, or cream-colored stem with a conical, honeycombed, or pitted cap. It grows on the ground in temperate and boreal parts of North America, Europe, and Asia, generally in disturbed places like burnt or logged woods, or next to dead or dying trees.

Morchella spp

-
- Its texture is crispy and meaty, while its taste is deep, earthy, and nutty. One of the most valuable and sought-after edible mushrooms, it has to be prepared before consumption since it contains toxins that might upset the stomach.
- **Truffle (Tuber spp.)**: This is a collection of mushrooms that grow underground in temperate and Mediterranean areas of North America, Europe, Asia, and Africa. They

often grow in symbiotic relationships with the roots of particular trees, such as oak, hazel, or pine. They are colored black, brown, white, or yellow, and their form might be rounded, uneven, or lobed.

Truffle Mushroom

- They are solid and waxy in texture, and they have a powerful, pungent, fragrant taste. These are among the priciest and most opulent edible mushrooms, and generally, it takes trained pigs or dogs to find them.

- **Chicken of the Woods (Laetiporus spp.)**: This mushroom has a structure like a shelf, fan, or rosette with a vivid orange, yellow, or salmon hue. It grows in temperate and subtropical parts of North America, Europe, and Asia on the trunks or stumps of hardwood or conifer trees. Its texture is soft and supple, and its taste is light, lemony, and chicken-like.

Laetiporus spp Musroom

- It is also well-known for having anti-inflammatory, anti-tumor, and anti-microbial qualities in medicine.

- **Oyster Mushroom (Pleurotus spp.)**: This mushroom has a small stem, or none at all, and a wide, fan-shaped, oyster-shaped cap. It grows in temperate and subtropical parts of North America, Europe, Asia, and Australia on wood, particularly hardwoods, in shelves or clusters. Its texture is velvety and smooth, and its taste is light, sweet, and nutty. It is also well recognized for its therapeutic qualities, which include raising immunity and reducing blood pressure, blood sugar, cholesterol, and blood sugar.

- **Chanterelle (Cantharellus spp.)**: This mushroom has a funnel-shaped, wavy, or lobed cap, and it may be yellow, orange, or apricot in color. It grows on the ground throughout the temperate and boreal areas of North America, Europe, and Asia, generally in close proximity to hardwood or conifer trees. Its texture is firm and chewy, and its taste is a combination of fruit, pepper, and nuts. This is a highly sought-after and delectable edible fungus; nevertheless, it should not be mistaken for the deadly Jack-o'-lantern (Omphalotus olearius).

The appearance and habitat of each mushroom

- **Lion's Mane (Hericium erinaceus)**:
- This mushroom has long, hanging spines that resemble cream or white pom-poms. It grows in the temperate woods of North America, Europe, and Asia on hardwood trees, particularly beech, oak, and maple. Its texture is akin to that of crab or lobster, and its taste is mild, sweet, and meaty. It is also well-known for its therapeutic qualities, which include strengthening the immune system, memory, and nerve regeneration.
- **Bleeding Tooth (Hydnellum peckii)**:
- This mushroom has crimson drips coming out of its pores, giving it the appearance of a tooth or sponge. It grows on the ground in temperate and boreal forests in North

America, Europe, and Asia, mainly under conifers. When young and fresh, it may be eaten, although it tastes harsh and peppery and might upset your stomach. Its ability to generate different hues of green, yellow, blue, and purple makes it more valuable for dyeing purposes.

- **Indigo Milk Cap (Lactarius indigo):**
- When sliced or wounded, this mushroom releases a milky or latex substance. Its cap, gills, and stem are all dark blue or indigo in color. It grows on the ground in the deciduous and mixed forests of eastern North America, East Asia, and Central America, mainly under hardwoods. Its texture is hard and brittle, and its taste is moderate, nutty, and somewhat sweet. It may be consumed pickled, cooked, or raw.

- **Latticed Stinkhorn (Clathrus ruber):**
- This mushroom starts out as a white, egg-shaped base and grows into a brilliant red, latticed or basket-like structure. It grows on the ground in warm temperate and subtropical parts of North America, Europe, Africa, Asia, and Australia, mainly on wood chips, mulch, or rich soil. Its greenish slime, which has an unpleasant odor, attracts flies and other insects, which aid in the spread of its spores. When it's young and still within the egg, it may be

eaten, but it tastes rubbery and bland and can make you sick or throw up.

- **Puffball (Basidiomycota)**:
- This category includes mushrooms without a cap, gills, or stem that are spherical, ball-like, or pear-like in form. They grow in a variety of habitats and places throughout North America, including on the ground, in wood, and in dung. When they are mature or disturbed, they expel the spores that are produced within their fruiting body in a plume of smoke. When young and white inside, they are edible; when old and yellow or brown inside, they become toxic. They are soft or spongy to the touch and have a mild, mushroomy, or nutty taste.
- **Morel (Morchella spp.)**:
- This mushroom has a hollow, white, or cream-colored stem with a conical, honeycombed, or pitted cap. It grows on the ground in temperate and boreal parts of North America, Europe, and Asia, generally in disturbed places like burnt or logged woods, or next to dead or dying trees. Its texture is crispy and meaty, while its taste is deep, earthy, and nutty. One of the most valuable and sought-after edible mushrooms, it has to be cooked before consumption since it contains toxins that may induce upset stomachs.

- **Truffle (Tuber spp.):**
- This is a collection of mushrooms that grow underground in temperate and Mediterranean areas of North America, Europe, Asia, and Africa. They often grow in symbiotic relationships with the roots of particular trees, such as oak, hazel, or pine. They are colored black, brown, white, or yellow, and their form might be rounded, uneven, or lobed. They are solid and waxy in texture, and they have a powerful, pungent, fragrant taste. These are among the priciest and most opulent edible mushrooms, and generally, it takes trained dogs or pigs to find them.

- **Chicken of the Woods (Laetiporus spp.):**
- This mushroom has a structure like a shelf, fan, or rosette with a vivid orange, yellow, or salmon hue. It grows in temperate and subtropical parts of North America, Europe, and Asia on the trunks or stumps of hardwood or conifer trees. Its texture is soft and supple, and its taste is light, lemony, and chicken-like. It is also well-known for having anti-inflammatory, anti-tumor, and anti-microbial qualities in medicine.

- **Oyster Mushroom (Pleurotus spp.):**
- This mushroom has a small stem, or none at all, and a wide, fan-shaped, oyster-shaped cap. It grows in temperate and subtropical parts of North America, Europe, Asia, and

Australia on wood, particularly hardwoods, in shelves or clusters. Its texture is velvety and smooth, and its taste is light, sweet, and nutty. It is also well recognized for its therapeutic qualities, which include raising immunity and reducing blood pressure, blood sugar, cholesterol, and blood sugar.

- **Chanterelle (Cantharellus spp.):**
- This mushroom has a funnel-shaped, wavy, or lobed cap, and it may be yellow, orange, or apricot in color. It grows on the ground throughout the temperate and boreal areas of North America, Europe, and Asia, generally in close proximity to hardwood or conifer trees. Its texture is firm and chewy, and its taste is a combination of fruit, pepper, and nuts. This is a highly sought-after and delectable edible fungus; nevertheless, it should not be mistaken for the deadly Jack-o'-lantern (Omphalotus olearius).

The special features and facts about each mushroom

- **<u>Lion's Mane (Hericium erinaceus)</u>**: This mushroom has several special features and facts, such as:

- It is sometimes referred to as the monkey head mushroom, hedgehog mushroom, bearded tooth, or pom pom mushroom.
- Being one of the few mushrooms that may promote nerve development and repair, it may be used to cure or prevent neurodegenerative illnesses like Parkinson's and Alzheimer's.
- It has a number of bioactive substances with anti-inflammatory, antioxidant, antibacterial, antiviral, and anticancer effects, including erinacines, hericenones, and beta-glucans.
- It may be grown both indoors and outdoors on a variety of substrates, including sawdust, straw, or logs.
- It may be used to create soups, sauces, and teas in addition to being cooked in a variety of ways, such as sautéing, frying, baking, or grilling.

- **<u>Bleeding Tooth (Hydnellum peckii)</u>**: This mushroom has several special features and facts, such as:
  - Other names for it include devil's teeth, red-juice tooth, and strawberries and cream.
  - It belongs to the family Bankeraceae, which also contains other toothed fungi like hedgehog and

cauliflower mushrooms, rather than being a genuine tooth fungus.

- o It generates a red pigment known as atromentin, which functions as an anticoagulant and is related to the blood thinner heparin.
- o Additionally, it yields pulvinic acid, a blue pigment with antibacterial and antioxidant qualities that may be utilized as a natural dye.
- o It is classified as a mycorrhizal fungus, which implies that it coexists symbiotically with the roots of several plants, including spruce, pine, and fir.

- **<u>Indigo Milk Cap (Lactarius indigo)</u>**: This mushroom has several special features and facts, such as:
    - o Blue cheese mushroom, blue lactarius, and blue milk mushroom are some other names for it.
    - o It is a member of the Lactarius genus, which is also home to other varieties of milk cap mushrooms, including green, caramel, and saffron.
    - o When broken or injured, it yields a blue latex or milk that oxidizes to become green, yellow, and finally brown.
    - o Its blue hue comes from a chemical called azulene, which also acts as an analgesic and anti-inflammatory.

- o It is regarded as a premium edible fungus and is often used in Mexican cooking under the names queso de monte and queso azul.

- **Latticed Stinkhorn (Clathrus ruber)**: This mushroom has several special features and facts, such as :
  - o It is also referred to as a lattice fungus, red cage, or basket stinkhorn.
  - o It is a member of the Phallales order of stinkhorn mushrooms, which also includes the dog stinkhorn, octopus stinkhorn, and devil's fingers.
  - o It releases a greenish slime, called gleba, that smells bad and contains its spores. Flies and other insects are drawn to the slime, which aids in the spores' dispersal.
  - o As a saprobic fungus, it consumes dead or decomposing organic materials, including compost, mulch, and wood chips.
  - o When it's young and still within the egg, it may be eaten, but it tastes rubbery and bland and can make you sick or throw up.

- **Puffball (Basidiomycota)**: This is a group of mushrooms that have several special features and facts, such as :
  - o They go by the names earth balls, smoke balls, and earth stars as well.

- o They are classified into many genera, including Calvatia, Lycoperdon, Bovista, and Geastrum. These genera have a variety of puffball varieties, including gigantic, gem-studded, common, and star-shaped puffballs.

  - o When they are mature or disturbed, they expel the spores that are produced within their fruiting body in a plume of smoke. Certain spores may live for years, and certain puffballs have the ability to discharge billions of spores at once.

  - o When young and white inside, they are edible; when old and yellow or brown inside, they become toxic. Some puffballs have a form similar to that of the deadly death cap or destructive angel mushrooms when they are young.

  - o They may be used for producing tinder, playing games, healing wounds, bleeding, or infections, among other medical and cultural purposes.

- **<u>Morel (Morchella spp.)</u>**: This mushroom has several special features and facts, such as :

  - o Other names for it include pinecone mushroom, sponge mushroom, and honeycomb mushroom.

- It is a member of the Morchellaceae family, which also contains black morels, half-free morels, and false morels.

- Its top is hollow, honeycombed, or pitted, and the spores are formed in small pits called asci. The species and environment will determine the color of the cap, which may range from yellow to tan to brown to black.

- It is highly valued and coveted among edible mushrooms, with a meaty and crunchy texture along with a deep, earthy, and nutty taste. Given that it contains toxins that may cause gastrointestinal upset, it must be boiled before consumption.

- It is classified as a mycorrhizal fungus, which implies that it coexists symbiotically with the roots of several plants, including apples, ash, and elm. It often grows next to dead or dying trees or in disturbed places like burned or logged woodlands.

- **Truffle (Tuber spp.)**: This is a group of mushrooms that have several special features and facts, such as :

  - They go by other names, such as subterranean mushrooms, white diamonds, and black diamonds.

- They are members of the Tuber genus, which also contains other varieties of truffles, such as summer, burgundy, white, and black truffles.
- They grow underground throughout the temperate and Mediterranean areas of North America, Europe, Asia, and Africa, frequently in symbiotic connection with the roots of particular trees, such as oak, hazel, or pine.
- They are solid and waxy in texture, and they have a powerful, pungent, fragrant taste. They are among of the priciest and most opulent edible mushrooms, and trained dogs or pigs are generally able to identify them thanks to their ability to detect their aroma.
- They stimulate the neurological system, increase blood circulation, and improve sexual function, among other medical and aphrodisiac qualities.

- **Chicken of the Woods (Laetiporus spp.)**: This mushroom has several special features and facts, such as :
  - Other names for it include chicken mushroom, crab-of-the-woods, and sulfur shelf.
  - It is a member of the Laetiporus genus, which also contains other varieties of chicken of the woods,

such the sulphur polypore, black-staining polypore, and white-pored varieties.

- o Its structure is rosette-like, fan-shaped, or brilliant orange, yellow, or salmon in color. It grows in temperate and subtropical parts of North America, Europe, and Asia on the trunks or stumps of hardwood or conifer trees.

- o Its texture is soft and supple, and its taste is light, lemony, and chicken-like. It is also well-known for having anti-inflammatory, anti-tumor, and anti-microbial qualities in medicine.

- o Some individuals may get allergic reactions or stomach issues from it, particularly if they consume it raw or undercooked or if it is gathered from eucalyptus or conifer trees.

- **Oyster Mushroom (Pleurotus spp.)**: This mushroom has several special features and facts, such as :

  - o It is also known as pearl oyster, tree oyster, or abalone mushroom.

  - o It belongs to the genus Pleurotus, which includes different types of oyster mushrooms, such as king oyster, elm oyster, phoenix oyster, blue oyster, pink oyster, and yellow oyster.

- o It grows on wood, especially hardwoods, in clusters or shelves, in the temperate and subtropical regions of North America, Europe, Asia, and Australia.
- o It has a mild, sweet, and nutty flavor, and a smooth, velvety texture. It is also known for its medicinal properties, such as lowering cholesterol, blood pressure, and blood sugar, and boosting immunity.
- o It can be cultivated on various substrates, such as straw, sawdust, or coffee grounds, and it can also be grown indoors or outdoors.

The ecological and conservation implications of foraging for exotic mushrooms

There are both advantages and disadvantages to foraging for exotic mushrooms in terms of the ecosystem and biodiversity preservation. Foraging for exotic mushrooms has the potential to improve the environment in the following ways:

- Promoting a feeling of stewardship and responsibility among foragers and the general public, as well as raising knowledge of the ecological significance and importance of mushrooms and their ecosystems.

- Lessening the strain on other natural resources and giving local populations, particularly those in remote and neglected places, an alternative and sustainable source of food, money, and livelihood.

- encouraging the preservation and restoration of natural forests, grasslands, and wetlands—all of which are home to a variety of exotic mushrooms—and the ecological services that these areas provide, such as soil fertility, carbon sequestration, and water purification.

- Helping to find new species and their possible applications, as well as advancing scientific knowledge and understanding of the variety, ecology, distribution, and interactions of mushrooms with other creatures.

However, gathering wild mushrooms may also have a negative impact on the ecology and preservation of biodiversity by:

- Trample, excavate, chop, or burn the mushrooms, their habitats, and the species that are connected to them, including plants, animals, and microbes.

- Reducing the amount of the mushroom population, its genetic variety, and its ability to reproduce by overharvesting, removing uncommon or immature individuals, or harvesting without allowing spores to regenerate.

- Moving or getting rid of contaminated goods, such as rubbish, timber, or soil, or using the wrong techniques or equipment may result in the introduction or spread of invasive species, infections, or pollutants.
- causing holes or edges that benefit opportunistic or competing species, or changing nutrient cycles, food webs, or symbiotic interactions in a way that disturbs or disrupts the ecological balance and ecosystem functioning.

Foraging for exotic mushrooms requires the adoption and observance of morally and environmentally sound methods, such as:

- Obtaining the required licenses, permissions, or permits from the appropriate authorities, landowners, or managers; and adhering to the guidelines for accessing, gathering, and using mushrooms and their environments.
- Learning about the ecology, identification, and preservation of mushrooms and their environments; and, when in doubt, especially when working with unknown or possibly hazardous species, consulting an expert for help or advice.
- Harvesting should only be done when necessary and permitted, allowing enough for the mushrooms' natural regeneration and the survival of the creatures that are linked with them. Rare or immature specimens should not

be harvested, nor should harvesting take place in bad weather like a cold or drought.

- Harvesting with caution and gentleness, making use of the right instruments and methods to minimize harm to the mushrooms, their environments, and the species that are connected with them (e.g., cutting or plucking instead of digging or tugging, and leaving the roots or mycelium intact).

- Before and after every foraging excursion, clean and sanitize the tools and equipment, dispose of any undesired or contaminated items in a safe and appropriate manner, and take care not to introduce or spread pollutants, diseases, or invasive species.

- Logging and reporting the observations and discoveries made during the foraging expeditions, disseminating the information and data to the appropriate authorities, groups, or researchers, and participating in the tracking and evaluation of the conditions and patterns of the mushrooms and their environments.

The ethical and cultural considerations for respecting the local traditions and communities

- Acknowledging the variety of cultures, the universality of ethics in a globalized society, and the symbolic, artistic, and historical significance of mushrooms and their habitats for many groups of people.

- Speaking of exotic mushroom foraging, it may affect the ethical and cultural aspects of regional customs and societies in both good and bad ways. Foraging for unusual mushrooms may be advantageous from an ethical and cultural standpoint in the following ways:

  - Acknowledging the significance of mushrooms and their habitats for many cultures and peoples, as well as their artistic, historical, and symbolic significance, while also honoring and valuing global ethics and cultural variety.

  - promoting a common ground to advance peace, justice, and human rights by enhancing communication, collaboration, and the sharing of information and experiences among many stakeholders, including foragers, landowners, managers, authorities, organizations, researchers, and educators.

o Respecting the rights, interests, and contributions of disadvantaged and Indigenous populations to the management and protection of mushrooms and their habitats, as well as promoting their empowerment and general well-being.

o appreciating and protecting the regional customs of harvesting rare mushrooms and respecting the ancient teachings and ideals of the Indigenous peoples, including courage, respect, truth, wisdom, humility, and love.

However, hunting for unusual mushrooms may also be detrimental to cultural and ethical elements of life by:

o generating moral conundrums and disputes amongst many stakeholders, including managers, landowners, researchers, educators, organizations, and foragers; as well as transgressing moral norms or values, such as accountability, justice, honesty, and respect.

o Disregarding or undermining the symbolic, artistic, and historical significance of mushrooms and their habitats for many cultures and peoples, as well as the variety of civilizations and universal morality in a globalized society.

- Rejecting or violating the rights, interests, and contributions of the local communities—particularly the Indigenous peoples and the disadvantaged groups—to the management and protection of mushrooms and their habitats, as well as exploiting or marginalizing them.
- Endangering or undermining the customs and traditions of the area, such as foraging for unusual mushrooms, and defaming the holy teachings and ideals of Indigenous cultures, which include courage, respect, truth, humility, knowledge, and love.

As a result, it's essential to embrace and adhere to moral and cultural foraging methods for exotic mushrooms, such as:

- Respecting the rights, interests, and contributions of the local communities—especially the Indigenous peoples and the marginalized groups—while actively seeking their informed permission, involvement, and cooperation in the management and protection of mushrooms and their habitats.
- Fostering communication, collaboration, and the sharing of information and experiences while

learning from and engaging with the many stakeholders—including educators, landowners, managers, authorities, organizations, researchers, and foragers—..

- appreciating and protecting the regional customs of harvesting rare mushrooms and respecting the ancient teachings and ideals of the Indigenous peoples, including courage, respect, truth, wisdom, humility, and love.

Part 3: The Advanced Topics of Mushroom Foraging

Chapter 7: How to Grow Your Own Mushrooms at Home

One of the planet's most interesting and varied species are mushrooms. They offer a diverse spectrum of nutritional advantages and ecological purposes, and they are available in an array of forms, sizes, colors, and textures. While some mushrooms are abundant and straightforward to locate, others are elusive and unusual. While some mushrooms are strange and exquisite, others arc straightforward and unremarkable. In this chapter, we will look at a variety of approaches and strategies for growing your own mushrooms at home. Growing your own mushrooms may provide you with fresh, healthy food and can be a fulfilling and fun activity.

The advantages and disadvantages of mushroom cultivation

There are a lot of advantages and disadvantages to growing mushrooms, depending on the kind, process, and volume of harvest. Among the benefits and drawbacks are:

Advantages

- Delicious and nutritious: With a range of tastes and textures to select from, mushrooms are a satisfying and healthy complement to any dish. They have no cholesterol and are minimal in calories, carbs, fat, and salt. Important nutrients like protein, fiber, vitamins, minerals, and antioxidants are also provided by them. Additionally, they may have therapeutic benefits that include boosting immunity, reducing blood pressure, cholesterol, and blood sugar, as well as preventing or curing a number of illnesses.

- Low maintenance: Growing mushrooms is a low-maintenance pastime or side business that takes little time or effort. The majority of mushrooms may be cultivated with basic or sophisticated equipment, in little or big places, and both inside and outdoors. They may also be produced without the use of dangerous chemicals or pesticides by using organic or recyclable materials like cardboard, sawdust, straw, and coffee grounds.

- Sustainable and environmentally friendly: Growing mushrooms may help the environment by raising consumer and producer knowledge of the importance of mushrooms to the ecosystem and their habitats, as well as by encouraging a feeling of stewardship and responsibility. It may also lessen the strain on other natural resources and provide local communities—particularly those in rural and underprivileged areas—an alternative and sustainable source of food, money, and livelihood. In addition, it may sustain the ecological services that natural forests, grasslands, and wetlands—where many mushrooms grow—provide, including carbon sequestration, water purification, and soil fertility. It may also aid in the identification of new species and their possible applications, as well as advance scientific knowledge and understanding of the variety, distribution, ecology, and interactions of mushrooms with other creatures.

- Space-efficient: Growing mushrooms is a lucrative and effective use of resources and space since it may produce a large number of mushrooms per square foot. Certain mushrooms may be cultivated in buckets, bags, or containers in tiny areas like a garage, basement, closet, or balcony. To make the most of vertical space, certain mushrooms may also be cultivated vertically on towers, shelves, or racks.

Disadvantages

- Initial outlay: Funding a mushroom culture enterprise might include a sizable upfront outlay for supplies and equipment, including spawn, substrate, bags, jars, tubs, steamers, flow hoods, thermometers, hygrometers, and so forth. Certain goods and equipment could be hard to locate or expensive to purchase, depending on their quality and availability. Over time, certain supplies and equipment could also need to be replaced or repaired, which would raise the cost of upkeep.

- Specialized information and expertise: Successful mushroom growing calls for specialized knowledge and expertise, which might be challenging for certain individuals to acquire. The requirements and difficulties associated with various mushroom cultivation techniques can vary. These include selecting the appropriate spawn and substrate, prepping and sterilizing the materials, inoculating and incubating the spawn, preserving the ideal humidity and temperature, harvesting and storing the mushrooms, and so forth. Certain oversights or errors might lead to crop failure, contamination, or infection, which could result in monetary losses or health hazards.

- Contamination risk: Bacteria, fungus, or insects may contaminate mushrooms, ruining a harvest and posing a health or financial danger. Any step of the growing process, including the preparation, inoculation, incubation, and fruiting of the substrate or spawn, may include contamination. A multitude of causes, including insufficient ventilation, inappropriate sterilization, poor hygiene, and environmental changes, may lead to contamination. By adhering to recommended measures, such as washing and disinfecting tools and equipment, utilizing sterile or pasteurized materials, working in a clean and isolated environment, and monitoring and modifying the circumstances, contamination may be avoided or minimized.

- Restricted variety: The range of mushrooms that may be cultivated is limited by the difficulty of cultivating particular varieties of mushrooms or their unsuitability for certain climates or situations. Certain mushrooms, for instance, could need certain substrates, temperatures, or light levels, which some growers might not be able to provide or find practical. The crop's quantity and demand may be impacted by the seasonal availability of certain mushrooms. Certain mushrooms, like psilocybin mushrooms, which are prohibited in many nations, or truffles, which are protected by conservation laws in certain areas, may also be subject to ethical or legal constraints.

The materials and supplies for mushroom cultivation

Depending on the kind, technique, and volume of production, several materials and resources may be used for mushroom growing. Typical supplies and materials include the following:

- Spawn: The substance used to inoculate the substrate with live mushroom mycelium is called spawn. A variety of materials, including grains, wood chips, sawdust, or plugs, may be used to make spawn, depending on the species of mushroom and the culture technique. Spon may be produced at home using tissue cultures from mushrooms or purchased from commercial providers.

- Substrate: The substance that gives mushrooms their nutrition and structural support throughout their development and fruiting is known as substrate. A variety of materials, including cardboard, paper, coffee grounds, hay, compost, and manure, may be used as substrates, depending on the species of mushroom and the culture technique. To prepare the materials for inoculation, the substrate may be made by soaking, cutting, mixing, or pasteurizing the ingredients.

- Bags: Bags are the holding spaces for the substrate and spawn that allow moisture and air to circulate. Depending on the kind of mushroom and the culture technique, bags may be manufactured of a variety of materials, including polypropylene, polyethylene, or filter patch. You may make your own bags at home or get them from commercial sources. Simply use plastic bags or tubing and close them with tape, ties, or clips. Additionally, bags may have perforations, filter patches, or injection openings to aid with mushroom fruiting, inoculation, and ventilation.

- Jars: Jars are the holding spaces for the substrate and spawn that allow moisture and air to circulate. Glass, plastic, or metal may all be used to make jars; it just depends on the kind of mushroom and how it is cultivated. Jars may be manufactured at home using cans or empty jars and sealed with foil, rings, or lids. They can be purchased from commercial sources. In order to aid with the inoculation, ventilation, or fruiting of the fungus, jars may additionally have injection ports, filter patches, or holes.

- Tubs: Tubs are the holding spaces for the substrate and spawn that provide moisture and air exchange. A variety of materials, including plastic, wood, and metal, may be used to make tubs, depending on the species of mushroom and the culture technique. Tubs may be manufactured at home using buckets, boxes, or trays and sealed with liners, covers, or lids. They can also be purchased from commercial vendors. To aid in the mushroom's fruiting or ventilation, tubs may also have holes, slits, or vents.

- A steamer is a machine that heats, sterilizes, and eliminates pollutants and pathogens from substrate and spawn. A mushroom steamer may be constructed from a variety of materials, including plastic, wood, or metal, depending on the kind of mushroom and how it is cultivated. A steamer may be manufactured at home using pots, pans, or kettles heated on stoves, burners, or microwaves, or it can be purchased from commercial vendors. To keep an eye on and regulate the steam's pressure and temperature, a steamer may additionally be equipped with gauges, valves, or thermometers.

- Flow hood: A flow hood is an apparatus that prevents pollutants and pathogens from entering the work area by creating a laminar flow of clean air using a fan and filter. A variety of materials, including plastic, wood, and metal, may be used to construct a flow hood, depending on the species of mushroom and the culture technique. A flow hood may be constructed at home using boxes, ducts, or pipes and connected with fans, filters, or switches. It can be purchased from commercial vendors. Add-ons like lights, timers, or alarms to a flow hood may help growers operate more efficiently and safely.

- Hygrometer: A hygrometer is a tool that determines the air's humidity or moisture content and aids in preserving the ideal circumstances for a mushroom's development and fruiting. A hygrometer may be constructed from a variety of materials, including wood, plastic, or metal, depending on the kind of mushroom and how it is grown. Hygrometers may be manufactured at home using a variety of supplies and techniques, including hair, metal, paper, or electrical sensors, or they can be purchased from commercial providers. A hygrometer may also be equipped with buttons, displays, or alarms to indicate and control the humidity level.

The steps and procedures for mushroom cultivation

Several typical actions and protocols include:

- Selecting a kind of mushroom to cultivate: Selecting the kind of mushroom you want to cultivate is the first stage, and it depends on your preferences, what's available, and appropriateness. Mushrooms may be cultivated at home in a variety of varieties, including oyster, shiitake, portobello, button, and morel. The needs and difficulties posed by various mushroom species vary, and include factors like spawn, substrate, temperature, humidity, light, and ventilation. Sproute or mushroom spores may be obtained commercially or online, or they can be harvested from spore prints or wild mushrooms.

- Growing media preparation: Also referred to as substrate preparation, this is the second phase in growing a mushroom. The substance known as the substrate gives the mushroom the nutrition and support it needs to develop and fruit. Depending on the kind of mushroom and the culture technique, the substrate may be constructed from a variety of organic materials, including straw, hay, cardboard, paper, coffee grounds, compost, or manure. To prepare the materials for inoculation, the substrate might be made by soaking, cutting, mixing, or pasteurizing them.

- Adding mushroom spawn to the medium: The third stage involves adding mushroom spawn—a substance that includes live mushroom mycelium—to the substrate. The whitish, thread-like network called the mycelium is what finally gives rise to the mushrooms by growing and spreading across the substrate. The spawn and substrate may be inoculated by stirring them together or by piling them in a container like a bag, jar, tub, or box. To avoid contamination or infection, the inoculation may be performed in a sterile and clean setting.

- The fourth stage involves incubating the inoculation substrate, which entails keeping it in a warm, humid, and dark place so that the mycelium may develop and colonize the substrate. The duration of the incubation period varies based on the species of mushroom and the growing technique, ranging from several days to several weeks. The incubation may be carried out in a specifically made chamber or room, or in a closet, garage, basement, or greenhouse. By sensing and modifying the environment's temperature, humidity, and ventilation, the incubation may be watched over and managed.

- Fruiting the colonized medium: In order to encourage the growth and creation of the mushrooms, the fifth step is to "fruit" the colonized substrate. Changes in the surrounding environment, such as a drop in temperature, an increase in light, or exposure to fresh air, might cause the fruiting to occur. The duration of fruiting varies based on the species of mushroom and growing technique, ranging from a few days to several weeks. It is possible to carry out the fruiting in the same location as the incubation or in a separate location, such as a shelf, rack, or tower. By monitoring and modifying the environment's temperature, humidity, light, and ventilation, the fruiting may be seen and managed.

- Gathering and preserving the mushrooms: Gathering and preserving the mushrooms for ingestion or trade is the sixth and last stage. Harvesting may be carried out by chopping or picking the mushrooms off the substrate, or by taking the substrate as a whole and leaving the mushrooms in place.

Depending on the species of mushroom and personal inclination, the mushrooms may be harvested at any stage of their growth. Harvesting may be done softly and cautiously so as not to harm the ground or the mushrooms. Depending on the variety of mushrooms and personal choice, storage options include freezing, canning, drying, and refrigeration. To stop spoiling or degradation, the storage may be done in a cold, dry, and dark environment.

Chapter 8: How to Join and Contribute to the Mushroom Community

In this chapter, we will look at how to become a part of and make a contribution to the mushroom community. The mushroom community is a group of individuals who are all passionate about mushrooms and their environments. Numerous advantages and possibilities, including learning, sharing, networking, cooperating, and having fun, may be found in the mushroom community.

The resources and organizations for mushroom enthusiasts

Mushroom aficionados may connect with other mushroom lovers, learn more about mushrooms, and take part in a variety of mushroom-related events and activities with the aid of several resources and organizations. Among the companies and resources are:

- Books: One of the easiest and most complete ways to learn about mushrooms is via books, which include information on identification, ecology, cultivation, culinary, medicine, and culture. Numerous publications are available to suit a range of interests and skill levels, from broad to specialized, and from novices to professionals. Among the well-liked novels are:

- David Arora's Mushrooms Demystified is a well-known and thorough reference book that has over, species of mushrooms along with thorough descriptions, images, and keys.

- Paul Stamets' groundbreaking and inspirational book Mycelium Running delves at the possible applications of mycelium and mushrooms in bioremediation, ecological restoration, and human health.

- The fascinating and educational book Entangled Life by Merlin Sheldrake explores the intriguing and hidden world of fungus and how they interact with other living forms.

- Anna Lowenhaupt Tsing's book The Mushroom at the End of the World explores the worldwide and local networks of the matsutake mushroom and its effects on culture, economics, and the environment. It is an engrossing and perceptive read.

- Websites: With a range of features and material, including blogs, podcasts, videos, forums, databases, and online courses, websites are among the most easily accessible and up-to-date places to learn about mushrooms. Numerous websites address various facets and interests related to mushrooms, including identification, cultivation, culinary, medicinal, and artistic interpretations. Among the well-known websites are:

- o Mushroom Observer: An interactive, community-based website where users may log in, share, and get comments on their observations of mushrooms from other users and professionals.

- o Fungi Perfecti: A reputable website offering knowledge and education on mushroom growing, ecology, and health, along with premium mushroom items including spawn, kits, supplements, books, and equipment.

- o The Mushroom is a lovely and educational website that offers a print magazine and an online community for those interested in mushrooms and those who deal with them to interact, exchange ideas, and find inspiration.

- o The World Mushroom Society is an association of health advocates and fungal aficionados that exchanges knowledge and identifies leading manufacturers of premium medical mushroom supplements.

- Organizations: Offering a variety of services and perks, including membership, newsletters, publications, seminars, lectures, field excursions, forays, festivals, and exhibits, organizations are among the most helpful and entertaining sources of knowledge and activities for mushroom lovers. Numerous organizations—local, national, or worldwide, general or specialized—serve various mushroom-related locations and scopes. Among the well-known groups are:

  o The non-profit North American Mycological Association (NAMA) supports the endeavors of more than 200 associated mushroom clubs and societies across North America and advances the scientific and educational aspects of mycology.

  o The Mycological Society of America (MSA) is a professional association that produces the book series The Fungal Community, the magazine Inoculum, and the journal Mycologia. It also works to promote and develop the field of mycology.

  o The biggest and oldest event of its type, the International Congress on Mushroom Science, is organized by the International Society for Mushroom Science (ISMS), an international organization that supports the cultivation, scientific study, and sale of edible mushrooms.

o The American Mushroom Institute (AMI) is a national voluntary trade organization that represents suppliers to the industry globally as well as American farmers, processors, and marketers of cultivated mushrooms.

The events and activities for mushroom lovers

Mushroom enthusiasts may find a wide range of events and activities to suit their interests and requirements, from recreational and instructive to creative and spiritual. Among the occasions and pursuits are:

- Foraging and mushroom identification: Foraging for mushrooms in the wild, whether for food or amusement, is one of the most well-liked and fulfilling pastimes for mushroom enthusiasts. In addition to helping mushroom enthusiasts appreciate the beauty and abundance of nature, mushroom identification and foraging may teach them more about the variety, ecology, and edible nature of mushrooms. Foraging and mushroom identification may be done in a variety of settings and throughout different seasons, by individuals or in groups, with or without guidance. Here are some pointers and safety measures for identifying and foraging for mushrooms:

- Always wear suitable clothes and footwear, bring a field guide, a basket, a knife, and a camera.
- Before visiting a foraging location, always check the weather, the terrain, and the authorization; furthermore, stay off of private or protected property and do not trespass.
- When harvesting and handling mushrooms, use extreme caution at all times. Additionally, stay away from touching or tasting any unfamiliar or toxic species.
- Before eating any mushrooms, always get advice from a professional or trustworthy source, and make sure they are cooked correctly.

- Growing and cooking their own mushrooms: Growing and cooking their own mushrooms, whether as a hobby or for health reasons, is another well-liked and satisfying pastime for mushroom enthusiasts. Cultivating and preparing mushrooms may enable connoisseurs to create wholesome, fresh mushrooms and explore many culinary techniques and dishes. It is possible to cultivate and cook mushrooms both indoors and outdoors, using a variety of tools and techniques, and with a range of kinds and variations. Here are some pointers and safety measures for growing and preparing mushrooms:

- o Use only premium mushroom spawn, substrate, and tools, and make sure you adhere to all the rules and specifications specific to the kind of mushroom you are growing.

- o Always monitor and regulate the temperature, light, and ventilation in the mushroom growth environment. Additionally, maintain it sterile, damp, and clean.

- o It is important to pick mushrooms at a mature but not overripe stage and store them in a cold, dry, and dark location.

- o Use fresh or dried mushrooms within a fair amount of time after washing and trimming them before cooking.

- Education and research on mushrooms: Learning more about mushrooms, whether for one's own or one's career, is a worthwhile endeavor for anybody who enjoys the edible plant. Education and research on mushrooms may benefit mycology enthusiasts by expanding their knowledge and expertise and advancing mycology's scientific and social standing. Research and education on mushrooms may be conducted on a variety of platforms and via a range of sources, including books, websites, online courses, workshops, lectures, journals, and projects. The following are some guidelines and safety measures for mushroom research and education:

- o Utilize a variety of sources and viewpoints, and always look for and confirm the reliability and caliber of the data and resources.
- o Respecting intellectual property and ethical norms, always reference and give credit to the authors and sources of the data and materials.
- o Always be observant and receptive, ask questions, and get input from knowledgeable people and other mushroom enthusiasts.
- o Always be analytical and imaginative, and use your knowledge and abilities to solve issues and produce new ideas.

- Spirituality and mushrooms: Expressing and exploring one's creative and spiritual side, whether for personal fulfillment or professional purposes, is a fascinating and fulfilling pastime for mushroom enthusiasts. A lover of mushrooms may transcend and establish connections with the world and themselves, as well as recognize and honor the mystique and beauty of mushrooms, via the medium of mushroom art and spirituality. Mushroom spirituality and art may take many different forms, including ritual, painting, photography, sculpture, music, poetry, and meditation. The following are some pointers and safety measures for spirituality and mushroom art:

- o Never use illegal or unsafe products or drugs, and refrain from hurting or upsetting other people.
- o Never force yourself on someone else or pass judgment on them; instead, respect and value the sensitivity and variety of cultures and individuals.
- o Share your voice and vision with both yourself and other people, and always be genuine and expressive.
- o Remember the holiness and wonder of mushrooms and life, and treat them with mindfulness and respect at all times.

The ways and means to share and learn from other mushroom foragers

How and where to exchange information and get tips from other mushroom foragers

Foraging for mushrooms is a fulfilling and delightful hobby that may improve your knowledge, well-being, and pleasure. But mushroom foraging may also be dangerous and difficult, particularly for novices or lone foragers. Because they can provide you with advice, encouragement, and company, other mushroom foragers are an invaluable resource. Share them and learn from them. There are several methods to communicate with and gain knowledge from other foragers of mushrooms, including:

Joining a mushroom club or society: A mushroom club or society is a group of people who organize and take part in various mushroom-related events and activities, such as field trips, forays, workshops, lectures, festivals, and exhibitions. It's one of the best ways to share and learn from other mushroom foragers. You may meet and connect with other mushroom enthusiasts by joining a club or society. These individuals can assist you with identifying, gathering, and preparing mushrooms, as well as sharing their knowledge, advice, and anecdotes. Participating in a mushroom club or society may facilitate your access to and contribution to the group's publications and resources, including books, periodicals, websites, bulletins, and magazines. You may advocate for the preservation and restoration of mushroom ecosystems as well as support the academic and scientific aspects of mycology by joining a club or organization dedicated to mushrooms. Numerous mushroom clubs and organizations exist, catering to various geographical areas and interests, including local, national, and worldwide, as well as general and specialized. Several well-known mushroom groups and clubs include:

- The non-profit North American Mycological Association (NAMA) supports the endeavors of more than 200 associated mushroom clubs and societies across North America and advances the scientific and educational aspects of mycology.

- The Mycological Society of America (MSA) is a professional association that produces the book series The Fungal Community, the magazine Inoculum, and the journal Mycologia. It also works to promote and develop the field of mycology.

- The biggest and oldest event of its type, the International Congress on Mushroom Science, is organized by the International Society for Mushroom Science (ISMS), an international organization that supports the cultivation, scientific study, and sale of edible mushrooms.

- The American Mushroom Institute (AMI) is a national voluntary trade organization that represents suppliers to the industry globally as well as American farmers, processors, and marketers of cultivated mushrooms.

Conclusion: The Joy and Reward of Mushroom Foraging

Foraging for mushrooms is more than simply a recreational activity. For individuals who follow it, a variety of advantages and possibilities may arise. We have looked at where to discover, recognize, and prepare edible wild mushrooms in this book, as well as how to get involved in and support the mushroom community. We shall consider the social and personal, ecological and environmental, and future and possible advantages of mushroom foraging in this last chapter.

The personal and social benefits of mushroom foraging

Foraging for mushrooms may improve your life in a lot of ways. It may provide you with wholesome and delectable cuisine, physical activity, cerebral stimulation, and emotional fulfillment, all of which can enhance your health, happiness, and general well-being. By enabling you to share your enthusiasm, expertise, and experiences with other mushroom enthusiasts and gain information from other viewpoints and ideas, it may help improve your relationships, connections, and interactions with other people. By establishing a connection between you and the greater mycological community as well as your culture and ancestry, mushroom foraging may also help you develop a sense of identity, purpose, and belonging. Foraging for mushrooms has many advantages for oneself and others, including:

- Health: Packed with vitamins, minerals, antioxidants, and other good stuff, mushrooms are a low-calorie, high-nutrient meal. They may decrease cholesterol, control blood sugar, strengthen your immune system, and prevent or cure a number of illnesses. Along with providing you with physical activity, fresh air, and sunshine exposure, mushroom foraging may also help to enhance your skeletal, respiratory, and cardiovascular health, as well as your mood and energy levels.

- Happiness: The distinct and nuanced taste and texture of mushrooms may enhance the richness and diversity of your meals and palate. Dopamine, serotonin, and other feel-good and joyful neurotransmitters may also be released when you eat mushrooms. In addition to testing your abilities and pushing yourself, mushroom foraging offers you the opportunity to take in the wonder and beauty of nature, as well as a feeling of fulfillment and success when you locate and gather your own mushrooms.

- Wellness: The complex and enigmatic qualities of mushrooms may uplift and enliven your mind and soul. Gaining information about mushrooms may pique your interest, broaden your knowledge base, and inspire your imagination and creativity. You may unwind and meditate while mushroom foraging, get away from the pressures and diversions of everyday life, and rediscover your inner tranquility.

- Relationships: The social and cultural importance of mushrooms may improve and reinforce your connections and relationships with others. Sharing mushrooms with your family and friends may create special and significant moments, as well as show them how much you care and how much you love them. You may also join and contribute to the mushroom community, which can provide you with resources, opportunities, and advantages, by going mushroom hunting. Foraging also offers you the ability to get to know and connect with other mushroom aficionados. These people can provide you with advice, support, and companionship.

- Relationships: The historical and ancestral significance of mushrooms might help you connect with and unite with your heritage. Understanding more about mushrooms may make it easier for you to respect and value your customs and history, as well as to recognize and cherish the richness and uniqueness of your culture and identity. In addition to allowing you to comprehend and value the ecological and environmental functions and interactions that mushrooms and other species play, mushroom foraging offers you the opportunity to establish a connection and speak with nature and its inhabitants.

- Objective: The educational and scientific value of mushrooms may inspire and enable you to work toward your ambitions. You may find and explore your hobbies and passions, as well as build and enhance your skills and talents, by studying mushrooms. You may also advocate for and support the preservation and restoration of biodiversity and mushroom habitats, as well as contribute to the growth and betterment of mycology and society, by going mushroom foraging.

The environmental and ecological benefits of mushroom foraging

Foraging for mushrooms has several positive effects on the ecology and the environment. In addition to promoting and enhancing the ecological roles and services of mushrooms as well as their interactions with other living forms, it may aid in the protection and preservation of the natural habitats and resources of mushrooms and other creatures. It may also aid in the creation and development of sustainable and regenerative alternatives and solutions for the future, as well as in minimizing and preventing the detrimental consequences of human activities and interventions on the environment and ecosystem. The following are some advantages of mushroom hunting for the environment and ecology:

- Protection: By increasing public knowledge of the importance and variety of mushrooms, as well as by promoting ethical and responsible harvesting and eating practices, mushroom foraging may contribute to the preservation and protection of the natural habitats and resources of mushrooms and other creatures. By generating demand and a market for their goods and services, as well as by offering incentives and rewards for their conservation and management, mushroom foraging may also contribute to the protection and preservation of the natural habitats and resources of mushrooms and other creatures.

- Promotion: By emphasizing and showing mushrooms' significance and potential in ecological restoration, bioremediation, and human health, mushroom foraging may assist in promoting and increasing the ecological functions and services of mushrooms and their interactions with other life forms. By supporting research and education projects and programs, applying and sharing the knowledge and skills gained from mushroom foraging, foraging can also help to promote and enhance the ecological functions and services of mushrooms and their interactions with other life forms.

- Reduction: By offering a low-impact and renewable source of food and medicine and by lowering reliance on and consumption of fossil fuels and synthetic chemicals, mushroom foraging can help to prevent and lessen the negative impacts and effects of human activities and interventions on the environment and the ecosystem. By utilizing and repurposing waste materials and byproducts, as well as minimizing and avoiding the generation and emission of pollutants and greenhouse gases, mushroom foraging can also help to reduce and prevent the negative impacts and effects of human activities and interventions on the environment and the ecosystem.

- Creation: By encouraging and supporting innovation and creativity, as well as by investigating and experimenting with new and unique applications and uses of mushrooms and their products, mushroom foraging may help to develop and promote sustainable and regenerative solutions and alternatives for the future. By working together with other mushroom foragers and stakeholders, as well as by influencing and engaging policymakers and decision makers, mushroom foraging may also help establish and promote sustainable and regenerative solutions and alternatives for the future.

The future and potential of mushroom foraging

Foraging for mushrooms is not only a worthwhile and pleasurable past time, but it also holds great promise and excitement for the future. Foraging for mushrooms may be a major and beneficial way to address and adapt to the many possibilities and difficulties the world confronts, including climate change, population expansion, food security, health care, and technological advancement. By extending and improving the range and quality of mushroom foraging, mushroom enthusiasts and the broader public may both benefit from the new and varied opportunities and experiences that come with mushroom foraging. The following are some prospective and future uses for mushroom foraging:

- Challenges: By monitoring and documenting the changes and impacts on mushroom populations and distributions, as well as by identifying and cultivating resilient and adaptable mushroom species and varieties, mushroom foraging can help to overcome and cope with the threats and challenges posed by climate change, such as extreme weather events, habitat loss, species extinction, and disease outbreaks. Foraging for mushrooms can also aid in overcoming and coping with the threats and challenges brought about by population growth, such as food insecurity, malnutrition, and poverty, by offering and promoting a cheap, wholesome source of food and medicine and by generating and sustaining opportunities for farmers and mushroom foragers to make a living.

- Opportunities: By increasing and improving the efficiency and effectiveness of mushroom identification, cultivation, and processing, as well as by creating and discovering new and creative products and applications of mushrooms and their compounds, mushroom foraging can help to seize and utilize the opportunities and benefits offered by technological development, such as artificial intelligence, biotechnology, and nanotechnology. By expanding and varying the availability and accessibility of mushrooms and their products, as well as by promoting and celebrating the cultural and individual diversity and identity of mushroom foragers and lovers, mushroom foraging can also aid in capitalizing on and utilizing the advantages and opportunities presented by social and cultural development, such as urbanization, multiculturalism, and globalization.

- Opportunities: For mushroom enthusiasts, mushroom foraging can present a wide range of fresh opportunities and experiences, including the chance to locate and sample novel and exotic mushroom species and varieties, travel to and explore previously uncharted territory for mushroom habitats, and acquire cutting-edge mushroom skills and techniques. The general public can also benefit from the new and varied opportunities and experiences that mushroom foraging can provide, such as recognizing and delighting in the beauty and wonder of mushrooms and nature, taking part in events and activities centered around mushrooms, and gaining knowledge and insight from mycology and mushroom experts.

Foraging for mushrooms is enjoyable and rewarding in and of itself, but it's much more than that. It is a means of fostering relationships with others, the natural world, and oneself. It's a means of supporting society, ecology, and the environment. It is a means of making the present and the future known and created. Foraging for mushrooms is a way of life and a way of love. We hope this book has given you the confidence and inspiration to start your own mushroom foraging trip as well as to get involved in and contribute to the mushroom community. It is our aim that you will locate, recognize, and prepare edible

www.ingramcontent.com/pod-product-compliance
Lightning Source LLC
Chambersburg PA
CBHW050805260726

48660CB00004B/1269